Daily Manna

God's Word of Blessing for You

365 Devotionals and Prayers
For Every Day of the Year

King James and New Living Translations

By Effell Williams, Sr.

Published by Effell Williams Ministries of Selma
PO Box 969
Selma, Alabama 36702

ISBN 978-0-9970914-4-1

Printed in the United States of America

For more information and other products
www.effellwilliams.org

To my wife, family, and church family for all of your support.
Continued blessings upon each of you!

DON'T GIVE IT PERMISSION

"Wherefore come out from among them, and be ye separate, saith the Lord, and touch not the unclean thing; and I will receive you."

2 Corinthians 6:17 (KJV)

Nothing can remain in your life without your permission. What you tolerate, you cannot reject or rebuke. Nothing can harm your call or purpose without you permitting it to remain in your life. It is not up to you who comes into your life; however, it is up to you who will remain in your life. You cannot be in the company of negative people and remain positive of the things concerning you. Don't allow negative people, thoughts, or opinions to remain around you. Remember, the scripture declares: "Blessed is the man that walketh not in the counsel of the ungodly, nor standeth in the way of sinners, nor sitteth in the seat of the scornful." To the best of your abilities, don't allow anything that will negatively affect your purpose and call to remain in your life.

Daily Prayer

Father God, please help me to remove any and all things that will negatively affect my purpose or call, in the Name of Jesus, Amen.

FAITHFUL

"Therefore, my beloved brethren, be ye stedfast, unmoveable, always abounding in the work of the Lord, forasmuch as ye know that your labour is not in vain in the Lord."

1 Corinthians 15:58 (KJV)

Getting to a particular place is half of the battle; staying there is the other part of becoming successful. Be steadfast in all that you are given to do, and remain faithful to your calling. The scripture declares: "The faithful shall abound in blessings." Don't be so concerned about how fast you get there, for staying there is the full reward. Apostle Paul declared: "Be not weary of well doing, for in due season, ye shall reap if ye faint not." The book of Revelation declares: "Be thou faithful unto to death, and I will give thee a crown of life." Remain steadfast, there are blessings and favor attached to doing so. Your legacy is produced by you remaining steadfast.

Daily Prayer

Father God, please help me to remain faithful and steadfast to what you have given me to do, in the Name of Jesus, Amen.

IN HIS PRESENCE

"Whither shall I go from thy Spirit? Or, whither shall I flee from thy presence?"

Psalm 139:7 (KJV)

God is always a present help in the time of trouble. He is never too far away to come to your rescue, nor will He be too busy to deliver you. The Psalmist declared: "I will dwell in the house of the Lord forever." You are never out of His sight or free from His Holy presence. King David declared: "If I ascend up into heaven, thou art there: if I make my bed in hell, behold, thou are there. If I take the wings of the morning, and dwell in the uttermost part of the sea; even there shall thy hand lead me, and thy right hand shall hold me." Rest today "in His presence, for in His presence is the fullness of joy and life evermore." He will be there today.

Daily Prayer

Father God, I thank you for always being a present help for me regardless of what I may face, in the Name of Jesus, Amen.

ACTIVE FAITH

"Thou believest that there is one God; thou doest well: the devils also believe, and tremble. But wilt thou know, O vain man, that faith without works is dead?"

James 2:19-20 (KJV)

Saying you have faith and actually having faith are two entirely different things. Remember, "Faith is the substance of things hoped for, the evidence of things not seen." If it is not put to work, can it really be faith? Apostle Paul declared: "I believed, and therefore have I spoken; we believe, and therefore speak." The Gospel according to Mark declared: "Whosoever shall say unto this mountain, be thou removed, and be thou cast into the sea; and shall not doubt in his heart, but shall believe that those things which he saith shall come to pass; he shall have whatsoever he saith." That's the faith James is referring to, for faith without works is useless.

Daily Prayer

Father God, help me to walk by faith, knowing that nothing will be impossible to me if I believe first, in Jesus' Name, Amen.

JUST ASK

"Ask of Me, and I shall give thee the heathen for thine inheritance, and the uttermost parts of the earth for thy possession."

Psalm 2:8 (KJV)

The Gospel according to St. Matthew declares: "Ask, and it shall be given you; seek, and ye shall find; knock, and it shall be opened unto you. For everyone that asketh receiveth; and he that seeketh findeth; and to him that knocketh it shall be opened." Never be afraid to ask God for what you want or need, for He is able to do exceeding abundantly above all that you can ask or think according to the power that worketh in you. There is nothing too hard for God to do; take Him at His Word. You have the invitation to ask, seek, and knock for what you want; and the Lord has promised that you could have it. It really is yours for the asking.

Daily Prayer

Father God, thank you for always being a prayer-answering God and for always being open to my requests, in Jesus' Name, Amen.

PROMISED PROSPERITY

"If they obey and serve Him, they shall spend their days in prosperity, and their years in pleasures."

Job 36:11 (KJV)

Know that it is the Father's will to bless you. In fact, 3 John 2 declares: "Beloved, I wish above all things that thou mayest prosper and be in health, even as thy soul prospereth." Job declared: "If they obey and serve Him, they shall spend their days in prosperity, and their years in pleasure." This is God's promise of blessings to you, no ifs or buts about it. He takes pleasure in the prosperity of His servants, and if this is His will for His servants, what do you think that He wants for His children? Decree today that nothing good will be withheld from me, in Jesus' Name. Go ahead. He said that you could decree a thing and it will be established unto you.

Daily Prayer

Father God, thank you for the favor and blessings that you will make available unto me throughout the day, in Jesus' Name, Amen.

GOD'S BLESSINGS

"So then they which be of faith are blessed with faithful Abraham."
Galatians 3:9 (KJV)

Every blessing that God promised to Abraham is yours also. Apostle Paul declared: "Christ has redeemed us from the curse of the law, being made a curse for us: for it is written, cursed is every one that hangeth on a tree: That the blessing of Abraham might come on the Gentiles through Jesus Christ; that we might receive the promise of the Spirit through faith." Yes, God has blessed you just as He did faithful Abraham. What were some of these blessings that God promised Abraham? He said, "I will make of thee a great nation, and I will bless thee, and make thy name great; and thou shalt be a blessing: and I will bless them that bless thee, and curse them that curseth thee: and in thee shall all families of the earth be blessed." You are included in this.

Daily Prayer

Father God, I claim all of the blessings that you promised to faithful Abraham, today, in the Name of Jesus, Amen.

SPIRIT LED

"A man's heart deviseth his way: but he Lord directeth his steps."
Proverbs 16:9 (KJV)

No matter what you plan to do, it is God who brings the plans to pass. The Psalmist declared: "Commit thy way unto the Lord; trust also in Him; and He shall bring it to pass." King Solomon declared: "Trust in the Lord with all thine heart; and lean not unto thine own understanding. In all thy ways acknowledge Him, and He shall direct thy path." How does He do this? Through His Word and the leading of the Holy Spirit. David declared: "Thy Word is a lamp unto my feet, and a light unto my path." The Apostle Paul even went further and declared: "For it is God which worketh in you both to will and to do of His good pleasure." So, it is God who gives you the plan and then the ability to carry it out. Trust Him today.

Daily Prayer

Father God, please help me to walk according to your Word and at the leading of the Holy Spirt throughout the day, in Jesus' Name, Amen.

DUE DILIGENCE

"Seest thou a man diligent in his business? He shall stand before kings; he shall not stand before mean men."

Proverbs 22:29 (KJV)

Scriptures declare: "The thoughts of the diligent tend only to plenteousness; but of everyone that is hasty only to want." King Solomon declared: "The hand of the diligent will rule, but the slack hand will be put to forced labor." He further stated: "I returned, and saw under the sun, that the race is not to the swift, nor the battle to the strong, neither yet bread to the wise, nor yet riches to men of understanding, nor yet favor to men of skill; but time and chance happeneth to them all." This means that regardless of the skills, abilities, intelligence, or strength, it is the faithful and diligent who achieve true and lasting success..

Daily Prayer

Father God, help me to remain diligent and faithful in the things that you have placed in my life, in the Name of Jesus, Amen.

HIS GRACE

"And the grace of our Lord was exceeding abundant with faith and love which is in Christ Jesus."

1 Timothy 1:14 (KJV)

Whatever you will face on today, Grace will be greater. Whatever you need today, Grace can help to provide it to you. The book of Hebrews declared: "Let us therefore come boldly unto the throne of grace, that we may obtain mercy, and find grace to help in the time of need." You will be given grace throughout the day without invitation or request. This grace is always sufficient, and His strength is made perfect in weakness. You do not have to worry, you are covered by this grace, regardless of what you will face, do, or be tempted to do. Submit to His will on today and enjoy the blessings that grace has purchased for you.

Daily Prayer

Father God, thank you for your amazing grace; grace that covers me throughout the day, in the Name of Jesus, Amen.

GOD'S CHOICE

"And have ye not read this scripture; The stone which the builders rejected is become the head of the corner."

Mark 12:10 (KJV)

God has not nor will He allow the rejection of some to stop you from fulfilling your God-ordained purpose. Some will reject you, some will distract you, and some will even overlook you. However, God has already declared your end from the beginning; and rejections, overlooks, and distractions have all been included in this plan. Remember, the Lord promised in Jeremiah: "For I know the thoughts that I think toward you, saith the Lord, thoughts of peace and not of evil, to give you an expected end." This will nullify the rejections of man and his efforts to short circuit God's will and purpose for your day. Always remember that if God is for you, who can be against you?

Daily Prayer

Father God, thank you for always being my source of all that I will need on today, in the Name of Jesus, Amen.

SOUND SPEECH

"A man's belly shall be satisfied with the fruit of his mouth; and with the increase of his lips shall he be filled."

Proverbs 18:20 (KJV)

Scripture urges us "not to make rash promises and don't be hasty in bringing matters before God. After all, God is in heaven, and you are here on earth. So, let your words be few." Moreover, by our words we will be justified, and by our words we will be condemned. Yes, "Wise words satisfy like a good meal; the right words bring satisfaction. The tongue can bring death or life; those who love to talk will reap the consequences." One could see life as a restaurant, and our words are like the menu. We receive what we order! The chef can only prepare what we order. What will you order today? Choose life.

Daily Prayer

Father God, help me to guard my tongue that I might not utter anything that may be harmful to me or others around me, in Jesus' Name, Amen.

RECEIVING THE IMPOSSIBLE

"Ah Lord God! Behold, thou hast made the heaven and the earth by Thy great power and stretched out arm, and there is nothing too hard for thee."
Jeremiah 32:17 (KJV)

Apostle Paul stated: "Now unto Him that is able to do exceeding abundantly above all that we ask or think, according to the power that worketh in us, unto Him be glory in the church by Christ Jesus throughout all ages, world without end." There is nothing too difficult or too hard for the Lord God to do. Your needs will not be too big, your requests will not be too numerous, nor your problems too great for the Lord to give you a successful day. Apostle John declared: "Ye are of God, little children, and have overcome them: because greater is He that is in you, than he that is in the world." There is nothing too hard for God to do on today – trust Him.

Daily Prayer

Father God, I know that nothing is too difficult or hard for you to do, and I am putting all of my trust in you for my successful day, in the Name of Jesus, Amen.

GODLY POSITION

"Thou wilt shew me the path of life: in Thy presence is fulness of joy; at Thy right hand there are pleasures for evermore."

Psalm 16:11 (KJV)

It is in the presence of the Lord that we find peace, joy, and true happiness. The enemy will fight you every step of the way to prevent you from entering into the Lord's presence. In the Gospel, Martha and Mary were entertaining Jesus at their home, and Martha was busy doing and preparing things at the residence. However, Mary was at the feet of Jesus listening to what He was saying. This disturbed Martha, and she asked Jesus to make Mary get up and help her; however, Jesus told her the following: "Martha, Martha, thou art careful and troubled about many things: but one thing is needful: and Mary hath chosen that good part, which shall not be taken away from her." This presence is not a one-time deal, but a lifestyle. Find your place.

Daily Prayer

Father God, thank you for your peace that you give unto me on a daily basis. Please help me to always trust in the leading of the Holy Spirit in all that I do, in Jesus' Name, Amen.

SAFE DWELLING

"He shall cover thee with His feathers, and under His wings shalt thou trust: His truth shall be thy shield and buckler."

Psalm 91:4 (KJV)

You have the assurance of God's protection and provision all day. He will never forsake or leave you. The Psalmist declared: "For thou hast been a shelter for me, and a strong tower from the enemy." Also, "The Name of the Lord is a strong tower: the righteous runneth into it, and is safe." You are covered by His grace, mercy, favor, and strength every day. The Prophet Isaiah declared: "Fear thou not; for I am with thee: be not dismayed; for I am thy God: I will strengthen thee; yea, I will help thee; yea, I will uphold thee with the right hand of my righteousness." David declared: "But thou, O Lord, art a shield for me; my glory, and the lifter up of mine head." Trust Him today to meet all of your needs and to protect you from the attacks of your enemy.

Daily Prayer

Father God, thank you for protecting me from the attacks of the enemy and from all that would harm me on today, in the Name of Jesus, Amen.

DELIVERANCE

"Evening, and morning, and at noon, will I pray, and cry aloud: and He shall hear my voice. He hath delivered my soul in peace from the battle that was against me: for there were many with me."

Psalm 55:17-18 (KJV)

The Lord spoke through the Prophet Isaiah: "No weapon that is formed against you shall prosper." This includes plans, traps, schemes, and all intentions of the enemy. David declared: "The Lord is my light and my salvation; whom shall I fear? The Lord is the strength of my life; of whom shall I be afraid? When the wicked, even mine enemies and my foes, came upon me to eat up my flesh they stumbled and fell." We are reminded in the Book of Psalm that "the salvation of the righteous is of the Lord: He is their strength in the time of trouble. And the Lord shall help them, and deliver them: He shall deliver them from the wicked, and save them, because they trust in Him."

Daily Prayer

Father God, I thank you for being my strong tower and for always being my shelter, in the Name of Jesus, Amen.

STRONG FINISH

"Know ye not that they which run in a race run all, but one receiveth the prize? So run, that ye may obtain."

1 Corinthians 9:24 (KJV)

It's not necessarily how you start but how you end that determines your legacy. You may start slow, but it's how you finish that will bring you the prize. The one who starts out first is not always the winner, but the one who is ahead at the end of the race receives the crown. Paul is encouraging us to "run that we might obtain the prize, not just to compete." He said "I run. Not as uncertainly; so fight I, not as one that beateth the air." God will grace you for what He has called you to do and will enable you to run in a manner that will cause you to win. God will empower you to run to win every time. Trust Him for all the instructions for your race today

Daily Prayer

Father God, teach me how to run my race with patience, looking unto Jesus, the author and finisher of my faith, in His Name, Amen.

OVERCOMER

"Now know I that the Lord saveth His anointed; He will hear him from His holy heaven with the saving strength of His right hand."

Psalm 20:6 (KJV)

David declared: "He delivered me from mine enemies: yea, thou liftest me up above those that rise up against me: thou hast delivered me from the violent man. I sought the Lord, and He heard me, and delivered me from all my fears." No matter what you face on today, God has promised to never leave nor forsake you. He is a present help in time of trouble. The enemy can try all that he can to distract, destroy, or block you on today; however, you can rest assured that when the enemy comes in like a flood, the Lord's Spirit will lift up a standard against him. Yes, you will not be left alone to try to defeat the enemy on your own. God will be there.

Daily Prayer

Father God, thank you for delivering me out of all my fears on today, in Jesus' Name, Amen.

DECREE IT

"I will declare the decree: the Lord hath said unto me, Thou art my Son; this day have I begotten thee."

Psalm 2:7 (KJV)

Speak today what you would like to come to pass on your behalf. Decree that nothing good will be withheld from me on today. You have death and life in the power of your tongue. Job declared: "Thou shalt also decree a thing and it shall be established unto you." Know that God has made heaven's resources available to us here on earth. We are told to pray "Thy Kingdom come, Thy will be done in earth as it is in heaven." Declare what you want, and have no doubt that God will bring great opportunities and blessings to you on today. Decree it today, regardless of what will face you on today.

Daily Prayer

Father God, thank you that you have given me the power to speak those things that be not as though they were, in the Name of Jesus, Amen.

EMPOWERED

"That being justified by His grace, we should be made heirs according to the hope of eternal life."

Titus 3:7 (KJV)

God's grace is simply amazing. He knows when to show up, when to empower, and when to lift. In fact, you are saved by grace, kept by grace, and empowered by this same grace. The Lord's Grace is sufficient for every need, weakness, disappointment, and any failures that concern you. Will it be easy? Maybe not; however, grace will be there to assist you in any manner necessary. No worries, for this grace will be there for you – on time, in time, and every time. No invitation necessary. Yes, this grace is sufficient and will be with you in the good times, in the bad times, and in everything. All you need to do is the receive Grace and allow it to operate freely in your life.

Daily Prayer

Father God, I thank you for keeping me, guiding me, and protecting me through all that will confront me, in the Name of Jesus, Amen.

LIMITLESS POWER

"Now unto Him that is able to do exceeding abundantly above all that we ask or think, according to the power that worketh in us."

Ephesians 3:20 (KJV)

Don't be afraid to ask for it; God is able. Don't be afraid to seek it; God can deliver it to you. Nothing is too big, too numerous, too large; nothing is impossible for God to do. He is able to do exceeding abundantly above all that we ask or think; therefore, you cannot ask too much or even think too much that will be beyond God's ability to do it. The Psalmist declared: "Trust in the Lord, and do good; so shalt thou dwell in the land, and verily thou shalt be fed. Delight thyself in the Lord; and He shall give thee the desires of thine heart. Commit thy way unto the Lord; trust also in Him; and He shall bring it to pass." Don't allow the moment to frighten you; God is always more than enough.

Daily Prayer

Father God, I rest in your power and grace for me every day, knowing that you are always more than enough for whatever I am faced with, in the Name of Jesus, Amen.

PATIENCE

"But they that wait upon the Lord shall renew their strength; they shall mount up with wings as eagles; they shall run, and not be weary; and they shall walk, and not faint."

Isaiah 40:31 (KJV)

Waiting upon the Lord is never a punishment, a chastening, or correction; but it is a time for maturing and seeking God's direction and guidance. King David declared: "Wait on the Lord: be of good courage, and He shall strengthen thine heart: wait, I say on the Lord." To wait upon the Lord does not mean that you sit and do nothing, but it means to seek God in all that you attempt to do. Don't move without seeking guidance from the Holy Spirit, and never be moved by not getting an immediate answer. Know that the "vision is yet for an appointed time, but at the end it shall speak, and not lie: though it tarry wait for it; because it will surely come, it will not tarry. Wait, I say upon the Lord, and He shall strengthen thine heart.

Daily Prayer

Father God, teach me how to wait upon you before I attempt to do anything, in the Name of Jesus, Amen.

DISCERNMENT

"Either make the tree good, and his fruit good; or else make the tree corrupt, and his fruit corrupt: for the tree is known by his fruit."

Matthew 12:33 (KJV)

Be mindful of your surroundings, for two cannot walk together unless they be in agreement on what direction they plan to go. Anyone or anything that causes you to move away from your purpose or call should be dismissed from your circle. We are told to know those who labor among us. Failure to do so can cause us to walk in the company of the wrong people. Remember, "Evil communication corrupts good manners." Yes, a tree is known by the fruit that it bears, and people are known by the acts that they consistently do. The "thief cometh not, but for to seal, and to kill, and to destroy." Anyone who falls into either category should not be allowed to remain in your future plans.

Daily Prayer

Father God, help me to know those who labor with me that I may know their spirits, thereby not being led in the wrong direction, in Jesus' Name, Amen.

IN HIS HANDS

"And there came a man of God, and spake unto the king of Israel, and said, Thus saith the Lord, Because the Syrians have said, The Lord is God of the hills, but He is not God of the valleys, therefore will I deliver all this great multitude into thine hand, and ye shall know that I am the Lord."

1 King 20:28 (KJV)

Try your best not to allow the low moment to depress you or to cause you to want to give up and quit. There will never be a testimony without a test. James declared: "My brethren, count it all joy when ye fall into divers temptations; knowing this, that the trying of your faith worketh patience. But let patience have her perfect work, that ye may be perfect and entire, wanting nothing." When you have low moments or valley experiences, know that it is there that you will grow and mature for the Master's use. King David declared: "Though I walk through the valley of the shadow of death, I will fear no evil: for thou art with me; thy rod and thy staff they comfort me." He will be with you through every situation.

Daily Prayer

Father God, thank you for always being a present help for me in all that I encounter, in the Name of Jesus, Amen.

SEIZE THE MOMENT

"While it is said, To day if ye will hear His voice, harden not your hearts, as in the provocation. For some, when they had heard, did provoke..."

Hebrews 3:15-16 (KJV)

Capture the moment; take advantage of the opportunity; take hold of the situation and move at the leading of the Holy Spirit. Believe that the moment is not too big or too difficult for you to attempt. Decree today that "I can do all things through Christ who strengthens me." Yesterday is gone, tomorrow is not promised to you; therefore, take full advantage of today. Don't allow the enemy to cause you to make the same mistake the children of Israel did when they heard the Word of God but did not mix it with faith; therefore, what they heard did not profit them. Be swift to hear and ready to move at God's commands today.

Daily Prayer

Father God, please help me to develop an ear to hear you clearly that I may not miss what you are saying and doing in this hour, in Jesus' Name, Amen.

HUMILITY

"A man's pride shall bring him low: but honour shall uphold the humble in spirit."

Proverbs 29:23 (KJV)

Stay humble – it's the key to exaltation from the Lord. The Psalmist declared: "Promotion cometh neither from the east, nor the west, nor from the south. But God is the judge: He putteth down one, and setteth up another." Walk in humility, for it will lead to godly promotion. The Lord declared: "Whosoever shall exalt himself shall be abased; and he that shall humble himself shall be exalted." It is humility before the promotion and correction for walking in pride. Solomon reminds us that "pride goeth before destruction, and an haughty spirit before a fall." You have a promise from the Father that if you humble yourself, you shall be exalted. Take Him at His word.

Daily Prayer

Father God, help me to walk in humility that pride will not be found in my ways, in Jesus' Name, Amen.

ASSURED VICTORY

"The Lord is my strength and song, and He is become my salvation: He is my God, and I will prepare Him an habitation; my father's God, and I will exalt Him."

Exodus 15:2 (KJV)

Apostle Paul declared to the Corinthians: "Now thanks be unto God, which always causeth us to triumph in Christ, and maketh manifest the savour of his knowledge by us in every place." Paul said that God always causes us to triumph, always. What an assurance to you to have a successful day. Isaiah reminds us that "no weapon that is formed against us will prosper," and since it will not prosper, the enemy hast to be defeated on your behalf. You are more than a conqueror through Christ Jesus. Yes, the Lord is your strength, and when the enemy shall come in like a flood, the Spirit of the Lord will lift up a standard against him. You will win; receive it as done.

Daily Prayer

Father God, I thank you for causing me to triumph over all of my enemies, in the Name of Jesus, Amen.

OPPORTUNITIES

"Now will I rise, saith the Lord; now will I be exalted; now will I lift up myself."

Isaiah 33:10 (KJV)

This is the day that the Lord has made, rejoice and be glad in it. This day was made for you and not you for the day. His grace is sufficient, His mercy is everlasting, and His truth endureth unto all generations. Take advantage of today, for tomorrow will take care of itself. We are told in scripture: "Take therefore no thought for the morrow: for the morrow shall take thought for the things of itself. Sufficient unto the day is the evil thereof." The Lord will manifest Himself today on your behalf. He will show Himself strong on your behalf. The Word declares: "Let God arise and His enemies be scattered." God will be exalted in the earth; join in and give Him glory.

Daily Prayer

Father God, show yourself might on my behalf today; arise and let your enemies be scattered today, in Jesus' Name, Amen.

OVERCOMER

"My brethren, count it all joy when ye fall into divers temptations; knowing this, that the trying of your faith worketh patience. But let patience have her perfect work, that ye may be perfect and entire, wanting nothing."

James 1:2-4 (KJV)

You may have trials on today; however, know that God has already declared your end from the beginning. The Psalmist declared: "Many are the afflictions of the righteous, yet God does deliver them out of them all." You have God's assurance that no weapon that is formed against you will prosper, and you can do all things through Christ who strengthens you. Apostle John declared: "They overcame him, the enemy, by the blood of the Lamb, and the word of their testimony." If there is no test, there can really be no testimony. If God allowed it to get to you, it is for certain that He will see you through it. Abide in His grace and mercy all day..

Daily Prayer

Father God, thank you for enabling me to persevere through all that I have encountered, in the Name of Jesus, Amen.

DIVINE REVELATION

"Who hath believed our report? And to whom is the arm of the Lord revealed?"

Isaiah 53:1 (KJV)

Apostle Paul declared: "But as it is written, eye hath not seen, nor ear heard, neither have entered into the heart of man, the things which God hath prepared for them that love him. But God hath revealed them unto us by His Spirit: for the Spirit searcheth all things, yea, the deep things of God." God wants to reveal himself to you today, and how does He do this? Through His Spirit. God has a plan for you, and it will be revealed to you through His Spirit. He wants to reveal what He has in store for you and all that He plans on doing on your behalf. Believe the report of the Lord; it is for your benefit, and it is in your best interest. Decree today that "I am walking in revelation knowledge of the Lord and His Kingdom."

Daily Prayer

Father God, I believe what you have spoken over me and for me, in the Name of Jesus, Amen.

PROVISIONS

"But my God shall supply all your need according to His riches in glory by Christ Jesus."

Philippians 4:19 (KJV)

It is through Christ that we move, breathe, and have our being. He is the source of all of our needs. Regardless of the need, God is able to provide it. The moment will not be too big for God, nor the situation too great that God cannot bring you through. Always keep in mind that "God is able to do exceeding abundantly above all that you can ask or think according to the power that worketh in you." He will supply all of your need according to His riches in glory by Christ Jesus." There is absolutely anything too hard for God, nothing. Trust in Him with all of your heart, and do not be anxious for nothing on today. God is still your source, and He never runs out of provisions.

Daily Prayer

Father God, I look to you for all of my needs. Please help me never to forget to seek you first in all that I do, in Jesus/ Name, Amen.

GOOD COMMUNICATION

"Be not deceived: evil communications corrupt good manners."
1 Corinthians 15:33 (KJV)

Everyone should not be given access to your hearing, for those who do have this access will speak to your visions, dreams, and future. Guard your hearing, for it has a direct path to your heart. The enemy only comes to steal, kill, and destroy; and he will use words from anyone to make this happen. If faith comes by hearing, then doubt, fear, and a lack of faith comes from hearing as well; wrong hearing. What you hear constantly will soon become your language of choice; don't allow this to happen. Never give those who do not hold your values and wishes access to you hearing. If you do, your communication could become affected as a result.

Daily Prayer

Father God, help me to guard my hearing that I do not speak anything that will offend those in my presence, in Jesus' Name, Amen.

BENEFITS OF TRUST

"And the Lord shall help them, and deliver them: He shall deliver them from the wicked, and save them, because they trust in Him."

Psalm 37:40 (KJV)

Trusting in the Lord God will bring great benefit. This trust includes waiting for, seeking Him, and being led by the Holy Spirit. The Psalmist declared: "They that trust in the Lord shall be as mount Zion, which cannot be removed, but abideth forever." He further stated: "Trust in the Lord and do good; so shalt thou dwell in the land, and verily thou shalt be fed." God will deliver; it will not be too late, too early, or too slow. He is not slack concerning His promises, and in Him is yes and amen. Nothing the enemy can do is more powerful than what God has planned for you on today. The Lord is not slow to bless, late to deliver, slow to forgive, nor forgetful of His promises.

Daily Prayer

Father God, I put my trust in you, please never let me be put to shame, in the Name of Jesus, Amen.

GOD'S MERCY

"But thou, O Lord, art a God full of compassion, and gracious, longsuffering, and plenteous in mercy and truth."

Psalm 86:15 (KJV)

Without question, God loves you unconditionally. In fact, Apostle Paul declared: "Nor height, nor depth, nor any other creature, shall be able to separate us from the love of God, which is in Christ Jesus our Lord." Because God's mercies are new every morning, you woke up this morning to new mercies. Scripture states, "Weeping may endure for a night, but joy cometh in the morning." His compassion fails not, and His mercy is everlasting. Declare today as the Prophet Isaiah stated: "And therefore will the Lord wait, that He may be gracious unto you, and therefore will He be exalted, that He may have mercy upon you; for the Lord is a God of judgement: blessed are all they that wait for Him."

Daily Prayer

Father God, thank you for your grace, mercy, and unconditional love that you have for me, in the Name of Jesus, Amen.

EXPECTACTIONS

"For unto us was the Gospel preached, as well as unto them: but the word preached did not profit them, not being mixed with faith in them that heard it."

Hebrews 4:2 (KJV)

Begin your day with expectations, looking unto Jesus, the author and finisher of your faith. Know that God can do all things, and nothing is impossible to them that believe. This is an unbelievable combination. Expectations should drive your requests, fuel your hunger, and give birth to new endeavors. David declared: "My soul, wait thou only upon God, for my expectation is from Him." Listen to the leading of the Holy Spirit today, and use your faith to deal with all that the enemy may throw at you. Remember, faith cometh by hearing and hearing by the word of God. Keep expecting the best and accept nothing less that comes your way.

Daily Prayer

Father God, please help me to walk by my faith and not by what I see with my natural eyes, in Jesus' Name, Amen.

NOW BLESSINGS

"Behold, I will do a new thing; now it shall spring forth; shall ye not know it? I will even make a way in the wilderness, and rivers in the desert."

Isaiah 43:19 (KJV)

This is your new day, regardless of yesterday's issues or problems. Today is a new day. Yesterday can be seen as a testimony to what you were able to go do; today is an opportunity for future success. Don't treat today as your yesterday; God has given you today for new opportunities and new beginnings. Today has a purpose; ask God for help in fulfilling your purpose. It will be through Christ and because of Christ that you will be successful. The anointing is on you, in you, and with you, making sure that you have everything you need to succeed. Whether or not you fulfilled your purpose for yesterday, today is a new moment, a new opportunity, one where yesterday is not important. Remember, His mercies are new every morning. Take full advantage of these mercies.

Daily Prayer

Father God, thank you for my new day. Please help me to take full advantage of its many benefits, in Jesus' Name, Amen.

BEST EFFORTS

"A slothful man hideth his hand in his bosom, and will not so much as bring it to his mouth again."

Proverbs 19:24 (KJV)

Solomon declared: "I went by the field of the slothful, and by the vineyard of the man void of understanding; and, lo, it was all grown over with thorns and nettles had covered the face thereof, and the stone wall thereof was broken down. Then I saw, and considered it well: I looked upon it, and received instruction. Yet a little sleep, a little slumber, a little folding of the hands to sleep: so shall thy poverty come as one that travelleth; and thy want as an armed man." The smallest deed that you can do is better than the greatest intention that you can have. Remember, you will reap what you sow; nothing sown, nothing to be harvested. To a large degree, today will be what you make it. Be diligent today to make something good happen.

Daily Prayer

Father God, help me not to be slack in my efforts today, that I may take full advantage of all that you make available to me, in Jesus' Name, Amen.

HIS WILL BE DONE

"And the world passeth away, and the lust thereof: but he that doeth the will of God abideth for ever."

1 John 2:17 (KJV)

The Apostle Paul declared: "For it is God which worketh in you both to will and to do of His good pleasure." This means that God not only gives you the will to do what He would have you to do but also the ability to do it. It's not our will but His will that we must make our priority. The will of God for your life is not changed, altered, modified, or withdrawn by the objections, plans, intentions or will of man. Why is this important? Because God "works all things after the counsel of His own will." The Book of Romans reminds us to "be not conformed to this world: but be transformed by the renewing of your mind, that ye may prove what is that good, and acceptable, and perfect, will of God." Let His will be done in your life today.

Daily Prayer

Father God, help me to abide not by my own will but by yours, in Jesus' Name, Amen.

ALL GOD

"Ask, and it shall be given you; seek, and ye shall find; knock, and it shall be opened unto you."

Matthew 7:7 (KJV)

It is through God, in Christ, that we move, exist, and have our being. In other words, it is through Christ that everything exists. Regardless of the report, The Lord is the final authority. No matter the need, nothing is too difficult for God to do on your behalf, for the Word declares: "Is there anything too difficult for me?" Christ Himself stated: "Everyone that asketh receiveth; and he that seeketh findeth; and to him that knocketh it shall be opened. Or what man is there of you, whom if his son ask bread, will he give him a stone? Or if he ask a fish, will he give him serpent? If ye then, being evil, know how to give good gifts to your children, how much more shall your Father which is in heaven give good things to them that ask Him?" Believe it and ask for it today.

Daily Prayer

Father God, I thank you that through Christ, I can do all that you will require of me on today, in the Name of Jesus, Amen.

THE LORD'S PROTECTION

"For the Lord your God is God of gods, and Lord of lords, a great God, a mighty, and a terrible, which regardeth not persons, nor taketh reward."
Deuteronomy 10:17 (KJV)

The Lord will never leave or forsake you. He is always a present help in the time of trouble. Regardless of the situation or circumstance in which you may find yourself, the Lord is greater; for greater is He that is in you than he that is in the world. King David declared: "The Lord is my light and my salvation; whom shall I fear? The Lord is the strength of my life; of whom shall I be afraid?" Those who oppose you are not able to defeat you, for Isaiah declared: "No weapon that is formed against thee shall prosper; and every tongue that shall rise against thee in judgment thou shalt condemn." These are not just words but promises from the Lord. Take Him at His word today.

Daily Prayer

Father God, thank you for my daily protection and guidance of the Holy Spirit, in the Name of Jesus, Amen.

MATURITY

"...Feed me with food convenient for me: Lest I be full, and deny thee, and say, Who is the Lord? Or lest I be poor, and steal, and take the Name of my God in vain."

Proverbs 30:8-9 (KJV)

You cannot mature into what God would have you to be without enduring some hardships, disappointments, setbacks, and other challenges. However, with them, you learn how to overcome. The book of Revelations declared: "And they overcame him by the blood of the Lamb, and by the word of their testimony; and they loved not their lives unto the death." The Lord will supply all of your needs according to His riches in glory by Christ Jesus. Pray as Christ instructed His disciples: "Give us this day our daily bread," depending upon Him for all of your needs, lifting up your eyes unto the hills from whence cometh your help, your help coming from the Lord.

Daily Prayer

Father God, thank you for seeing me through the issues that I may face and allowing me to mature as a result of them, in Jesus' Name, Amen.

HARVESTING

"Can a woman forget her sucking child, that she should not have compassion on the son of her womb? Yea, they may forget, yet will I not forget thee."

Isaiah 49:15 (KJV

Apostle Paul declared: "Be not deceived; God is not mocked: for whatsoever a man soweth, that shall he also reap." God is not slack concerning His promises made to you. Man may overlook you, forget you, or dismiss you, but God cannot forget who you are and what He has promised you. The Psalmist declared: "For the Lord God is a sun and shield: the Lord will give grace and glory: no good thing will He withhold from them that walk uprightly." As Isaiah stated: "Can a woman forget her sucking child, that she should not have compassion on the son of her womb? Yea, they may forget, yet will I not forget thee." The Lord will not forget you today, regardless of who else does.

Daily Prayer

Father God, please help me to keep watering my seed that I can receive the harvest promised to me, in Jesus' Name, Amen.

PATIENCE

"But let patience have her perfect work, that ye may be perfect and entire, wanting nothing."

James 1: 4 (KJV)

Patience is a maturing factor in your life like nothing else. The Hebrews writer declared: "For ye have need of patience, that after ye have done the will of God, ye might receive the promise." Yes, even after you have done all that is required, sometimes you still must wait to receive what the labor has promised. James declared: "My brethren, count it all joy when ye fall into divers temptations; knowing this, that the trying of your faith worketh patience. But let patience have her perfect work, that ye may be perfect and entire wanting nothing." Being patient beats impatience any day of the week. Remember, "They that wait on the Lord shall renew their strength; they shall mount up with wings as eagles; they shall run, and not be weary; and they shall walk, and not faint."

Daily Prayer

Father God, teach me how to wait for you for all that I need so that I do not get ahead of you, in Jesus' Name, Amen.

DEPENDENCY

"Wait on the Lord, and keep His way, and He shall exalt thee to inherit the land: when the wicked are cut off, thou shalt see it."

Psalms 37:34 (KJV)

Waiting on the Lord does not mean that you have to do nothing or be engaged in any activities, but it does mean that you will not do anything without the leading of the Holy Spirit. King Solomon suggests that we "trust in the Lord with all of our heart; lean not unto our own understanding; in all of our ways acknowledge Him, and He will direct our paths." Waiting on God means to defer to His will, not your own. The Psalmist declared: "Wait on the Lord; and keep His way, and He shall exalt thee to inherit the land: when the wicked are cut off, thou shalt see it." Remember to "Seek ye first the Kingdom of God and its righteousness, and all these things will be added unto you." Wait, I say, on the Lord.

Daily Prayer

Father God, I will wait on you for all that I need, desire, and want to do, in Jesus' Name, Amen.

GOD WITH YOU

"There shall not any man be able to stand before thee all the days of thy life: as I was with Moses, so I will be with thee: I will not fail thee, nor forsake thee."

Joshua 1:5 (KJV)

After Moses passed away, The Lord God chose Joshua to succeed him. Of course, this was a very difficult replacement, and God wanted to assure him that He would be with him as He was with Moses. Know for a certainty that whatever God has called you to do, He will see you through all the way until the finished line. Regardless of the enemy, as He said unto Joshua, the same applies to you: "He will not fail thee, nor forsake thee." In fact, He said in the Book of Isaiah that "behold, they shall surely gather together, but not by Me: whosoever shall gather together against thee shall fall for thy sake." Trust Him today to guide you through all the attacks of your enemies.

Daily Prayer

Father God, thank you for your divine protection that you provide for me on a daily basis, in Jesus' Name, Amen.

DIVINE TRUST

"Ye that fear the Lord, trust in the Lord: He is their help and their shield."
Psalms 115:11 (KJV)

The Lord will never fail to keep His word and promise to you. The Psalmist declared: "They that trust in the Lord shall be as mount Zion, which cannot be removed, but abideth forever." Yes, God is your helper and shield, and He will never forsake or leave you. King David declared: "The Lord is my rock, and my fortress, and my deliverer; my God, my strength, in whom I will trust; my buckler, and the horn of my salvation, and my high tower." Always remember that He changes not. He is the same yesterday, today, and forever. Even when we are faithless, He is faithful, for He cannot deny Himself. Yes, you can safely put your trust in the Lord; He is faithful.

Daily Prayer

Father God, I trust you with all of my heart and with all that I face today, in Jesus' Name, Amen.

STANDING ON THE PROMISES

"I have been young, and now am old; yet have I not seen the righteous forsaken, nor his seed begging bread."

Psalms 37:25 (KJV)

The Lord is not slack concerning His promises to you. He cannot lie, nor can He go back on His Word. Jeremiah declared: "I know the thoughts that I think toward you, saith the Lord, thoughts of peace, and not of evil, to give you an expected end" – a promise of a good ending. You will not be forsaken, for the mouth of the Lord has spoken it. You can be certain that God will do what He said in the safety of the Holy Scriptures. He declared in Hebrews: "For when God made promise to Abraham, because He could swear by no greater, He sware by Himself, Saying, surely blessing I will bless thee, and multiplying I will multiply thee." Yes, God is bound by His word to do what He has promised; rejoice today, for you are safe in His promises.

Daily Prayer

Father God, thank you for always being true to your word and the promises that I can stand on, in Jesus' Name, Amen.

RIGHTEOUSNESS

"For thou, Lord, wilt bless the righteous; with favor wilt thou compass him as with a shield."

Psalms 5:12 (KJV)

Each morning when you awake, you must remember that you are the righteousness of God through Christ Jesus. Apostle Paul declared: "For He hath made Him to be sin for us, who knew no sin; that we might be made the righteousness of God in Him." Because you are righteous in the sight of God through Christ, you can rest assured that on today, according to scripture, as the Psalmist did: "For the Lord God is a sun and shield: the Lord will give grace and glory: no good thing will He withhold from them that walk uprightly." Rest assured, you are the righteousness of God; therefore, the Lord has promised that you will not be forsaken, nor your seed will ever beg for bread.

Daily Prayer

Father God, I thank you for being made righteous in your sight through Jesus Christ, in His Name, Amen.

ASKING IN JESUS' NAME

"And whatsoever ye shall ask in My Name, that will I do, that the Father may be glorified in the Son."

John 14:13 (KJV)

Jesus said that we can ask the Father anything in His Name, and He would do it. Why? So that the Father would be glorified in the Son. Nothing is too big, too small, or too numerous for you to ask. In fact, Matthew stated: "Ask, and it shall be given you; seek, and ye shall find; knock, and it shall be opened unto you." You are at liberty to ask the Father whatsoever you will, in Jesus' Name, and have the confidence that the Son will do it to glorify the Father. He said, "If ye shall ask anything in My Name, I will do it." Whatever you are in need of, the Father has given you an invitation to come and ask in Jesus' Name, and the Son will do it that the Father be glorified.

Daily Prayer

Father God, thank you that I can ask anything of you through Jesus Christ, knowing with confidence that it will be done so that You will be glorified, in His Name, Amen.

DIVINE COVERING

"Thou art my hiding place; thou shalt preserve me from trouble; thou shalt compass me about with songs of deliverance…"

Psalms 32:7 (KJV)

Nothing you have or will face can compete with God's grace and mercy. He will cover you as with feathers; for the Psalmist declared: "I will say of the Lord, He is my refuge and my fortress: my God; in Him will I trust. Surely He shall deliver thee from the snare of the fowler, and from the noisome pestilence. He shall cover thee with His feathers, and under His wings shalt thou trust: His truth shall be thy shield and buckler." In His presence is the fullness of joy and life evermore. The Psalmist declared: "For in the time of trouble He shall hide me in His pavilion: in the secret of His tabernacle shall He hide me; He shall set me up upon a rock." Remain safe in Him all day.

Daily Prayer

Father God, thank you for covering me throughout the storms in my life and for being a shield for me against all my enemies, in the Name of Jesus, Amen.

BE LIFTED UP

"Why are thou cast down, O my soul? And why art thou disquieted in me? Hope thou in God: for I shall yet praise Him for the help of His countenance."

Psalms 42:5 (KJV)

The enemy will try to get you to be despondent, discouraged, depressed, and sad at your current situation or circumstance; however, you must try with all of your might to remind the enemy that God is your help, and your expectation is still in the Lord. Don't allow past mistakes, missteps, or failures to stand in your path to full recovery and success on today. God is not threatened by your past or current situation, and the door to His presence is still open to you. You cannot, nor will you ever be able to exhaust God's unconditional love, grace, or mercy. All are limitless. Don't be cast down; God is still your source for all that you need.

Daily Prayer

Father God, I place all of my hope and expectation in you, knowing that you will never forsake or leave me, in the Name of Jesus, Amen.

GOD'S GREATNESS

"Thine, O Lord, is the greatness, and the power, and the glory, and the victory, and the majesty: for all that is in the heaven and in the earth is thine; thine is the kingdom, O Lord, and thou art exalted as head above all."

1 Chronicles 29:11 (KJV)

There is none to be compared to the Lord our God, for "He is able to do ecxceeding abundantly above all that we can ask or think, according to the power that worketh in us." All power belongs unto Him, and nothing is too difficult for Him to do on our behalf. This greatness cannot be questioned, doubted, disbelieved, or dismissed. It can never be matched or equaled. Therefore, regardless of your problems, trials, or battles, you have the "Greater Than" on your side. Your life is not left to the wishes of the world, its system, or the plans of others. Know that He is the Lord of lords, King of kings, and the Great I Am; and He is on your side every single day.

Daily Prayer

Father God, thank you for always being more than enough for me, regardless of my situation or circumstance, in the Name of Jesus, Amen.

PREDESTINED

"Before I formed thee in the belly I knew thee; and before thou camest forth out of the womb I sanctified thee, and I ordained thee a prophet unto the nations."

Jeremiah 1:5 (KJV)

God is not making things up for you as you go along. He had plans for you before you were even born. He has no plan B for you because His plan for your life is the only one He needs for you to accomplish His purpose for your life. In fact, The Prophet Isaiah declared: "He declared your end from the beginning." The Apostle Paul made it clear when he said, "For whom He did foreknow, He also did predestinate to be conformed to the image of His Son, that He might be the first-born among many brethren. Moreover whom He did predestinate, them He also called: and whom He called, them He also justified: and whom He justified, them He also glorified." God has prearranged not only your future, but also this day. Follow Him, and you will succeed.

Daily Prayer

Father God, thank you for prearranging my day and my life. Please help me to walk in the plans and purpose that you have for me today, in Jesus' Name, Amen.

FAITH THAT WORKS

"And Jesus said unto them, Because of your unbelief: for verily I say unto you, if ye have faith as a grain of a mustard seed, ye shall say unto this mountain, Remove hence to yonder place; and it shall remove; and nothing shall be impossible unto you."

Matthew 17:20 (KJV)

Jesus said that nothing is impossible to them that believe, nothing! Job declared: "Thou shalt also decree a thing, and it shall be established unto thee: and the light shall shine upon thy ways." In the Gospel according to Mark, Jesus says, "Have faith in God. For verily I say unto you, that whosoever shall say unto this mountain, be thou removed, and be thou cast into the sea; and shall not doubt in his heart, but shall believe that those things which he saith shall come to pass; he shall have whatsoever he saith. Therefore, I say unto you, What things soever ye desire, when ye pray, believe that ye receive them, and ye shall have them." If you can generate the faith, God is able to bring it to pass.

Daily Prayer

Father God, help me to walk by my faith and not by my sight in all that faces me, in Jesus' Name, Amen.

WALKING IN CONFIDENCE

"For the Lord shall be thy confidence, and shall keep thy foot from being taken."

Proverbs 3:26 (KJV)

God is your confidence; always faithful to His Word, His promise, and His plan for your life. God will not give you over to the will or plans of any of your enemies, and He knows what He is going to do in your life. Your confidence in the Father will keep you on solid foundation. The Book of Habakkuk declared: "The Lord God is my strength, and He will make my feet like hinds' feet, and He will make me to walk upon mine high places." It is always better to put your trust and confidence in God rather than in man. The Lord is faithful and is not slack concerning His promises to you. You can go throughout the day knowing that God's grace will empower you; His mercy shall cover you, and His love for you will far outweigh any evil that the enemy tries to put on you.

Daily Prayer

Father God, I place all of my confidence in You, Your Word, and the Holy Spirit to direct me throughout the day, in Jesus' Name, Amen.

OVERCOMER

"Ye are of God, little children, and have overcome them: because greater is He that is in you, than he that is in the world."

1 John 4:4 (KJV)

You are an overcomer because the Spirit of the Lord lives in you. In fact, Apostle Paul declared: "You are more than a conqueror through Christ that loves you." Regardless of the enemy, God is greater, and He has declared that no weapon that is formed against you will prosper. The Word of God lets us know that whatever God gives birth to will overcome; for He is the Alpha and Omega of our lives, the beginning and the end of our purpose. People can frustrate our purpose, but they cannot stop it from coming to pass. Anything God-given will be God-protected. He will come through for you on time and in time; just don't lose hope in the Lord God. He will renew your strength and always cause you to triumph.

Daily Prayer

Father God, thank you for always causing me to triumph through Christ Jesus, in His Name, Amen.

GOOD FIGHT OF FAITH

"Fight the good fight of faith, lay hold on eternal life, whereunto thou art also called, and hast professed a good profession before many witnesses."

1 Timothy 6:12 (KJV)

We are told to fight the good fight of faith, and to contend for the same. We have an adversary who goes about seeking whom he may devour. Fight through the Spirit to do what is right; fight for new revelation; fight for the call; fight for new heights in the Lord. Keep fighting until the victory is won. There are no other options. Believe what God has said about you, and give no thought to what "they" think about you. It will serve no good purpose. You are fearfully and wonderfully made in His image and likeness. The frustration that the enemy may cause is only temporary, but God's will for you is permanent. Trust Him today, and keep up your fight.

Daily Prayer

Father God, help me to be strong in the Spirit and to keep fighting the good fight of faith, in Jesus' Name, Amen.

SAVED IN CHRIST

"For in the time of trouble He shall hide me in His pavilion: in the secret of His tabernacle shall He hide me; He shall set me up upon a rock."

Psalms 27:5 (KJV)

What a blessing to wake up every morning to the fact that God will always be on our side protecting, providing, and leading us throughout the day. Declare and decree today that "The Lord is my light and my salvation; whom shall I fear? The Lord is the strength of my life; of whom shall I be afraid?" He is, today and always, a present help in the time of trouble. We don't have to worry about God doing what He promised; we just have to do those things that are pleasing in His sight to receive the promises. He never has to be reminded of what He said or promised to us. We can be assured of this help every day, for His mercies are new every morning.

Daily Prayer

Father God, thank you for allowing me to experience your awesome presence every day and for allowing me to trust in you for all that I need, in Jesus' Name, Amen.

BY MY TESTIMONY

"Quicken me after thy lovingkindness; so shall I keep the testimony of thy mouth."

Psalms 119:88 (KJV)

Today, regardless of the things that will confront you, you have a testimony of God's amazing grace in your life. You can look back and see all that God has done for you and how He caused you to triumph over your enemies. If need be, remind your enemies that if God did that for me, He will surely take me through this as well. The scripture states: "And they overcame him by the blood of the Lamb, and by the word of their testimony; and they loved not their lives unto the death." Also, "Remember His marvelous works that He hath done, His wonders, and the judgements of His mouth." You are an overcomer, and nothing the enemy can bring to you can change this fact.

Daily Prayer

Father God, thank you for all that you have brought me through, giving me a testimony to use against the enemy's attacks, in Jesus' Name, Amen.

HIS COUNSEL

"In whom also we have obtained an inheritance, being predestinated according to the purpose of Him who worketh all things after the counsel of His own will."

Ephesians 1:11 (KJV)

It's not so much what you face but who is in the situation or circumstance with you. Whatever God brings you to, know for a certainty that He is able to bring you through it as well. As a believer, don't be afraid and don't be dismayed, but know that "man's ways are not God's ways, and man's thoughts are not God's thoughts; for as the heavens are higher than the earth, so are God's ways than our ways, and God's thoughts than our thoughts." We will survive and thrive. Know that the same God who brought you out can also keep you out. God worketh all things after the counsel of His own will, not man's. Be encouraged.

Daily Prayer

Father God, thank you that I can trust in the plans and purpose that you have for me, in the Name of Jesus, Amen.

TOTAL DEPENDENCY

"Now unto Him that is able to keep you from falling, and to present you faultless before the presence of His glory with exceeding joy, to the only wise God our Savior, be glory and majesty, dominion and power, both now and ever. Amen."

Jude 24-25 (KJV)

No matter what, God is always the same! He changes not; and if He did "it" before, remind your enemy that He can do it again. Be confident and assured that He is for you today, tomorrow, and in the future. He knows how to keep you. He is God, and He changes not. He is the same yesterday, today, and forever. All that confronts you will come as no surprise to Him. His grace does not need an invitation to become active in your life. You will not have to look for Him, wait for Him, nor beg Him. God is always a present help in the time of trouble. He is able to keep you from falling, and to present you faultless before the presence of his glory – trust Him.

Daily Prayer

Father God, thank you for keeping me from all that would do me harm today, in the Name of Jesus, Amen.

DIVINE LIBERTY

"Stand fast therefore in the liberty wherewith Christ hath made us free, and be not entangled again with the yoke of bondage."

Galatians 5:1 (KJV)

Whom the Son sets free is free indeed. The Gospel of John declared: "And ye shall know the truth and the truth shall make you free." Don't allow anything or anyone to cause you to slip back into bondage. You are free indeed. Apostle Paul declared: "And you, being dead in your sins and the uncircumcision of your flesh, hath He quickened together with him, have forgiven you all trespasses; blotting out the handwriting of ordinances that was against us, which was contrary to us, and took it out of the way, nailing it to His cross; and having spoiled principalities and powers, He made a shew of them openly, triumphing over them in it." You are free in Jesus' Name. Enjoy this liberty and freedom to the fullest today.

Daily Prayer

Father God, thank you for freeing me from all that had me in bondage and from all that would harm me, in Jesus' Name, Amen.

SPEAK LIFE TO IT

"(As it is written, I have made thee a father of many nations,) before him whom he believed, even God, who quickeneth the dead, and calleth those things which be not as though they were."

Romans 4:17 (KJV)

According to scripture, "Death and life are in the power of the tongue: and they that love it shall eat the fruit thereof." This is the authority that God has given to you as a believer. Job declared: "Thou shalt also decree a thing, and it shall be established unto thee: and the light shall shine upon thy ways." If the atmosphere is not what you need for your miracle, create your own, one that is more conducive for a miracle! Speak it, for you can call those things which be not as though they were." Don't wait for the perfect surrounding; create an atmosphere that is conducive for miracles, blessings, and increase to occur. Speak it.

Daily Prayer

Father God, help me to speak those things that be not as though they were so that I do not have to accept those things that are not according to your will for my life, in Jesus', Amen.

FOR HIS GLORY

"That the Name of our Lord Jesus Christ may be glorified in you, and ye in Him, according to the grace of our God and the Lord Jesus Christ."

2 Thessalonians 1:12 (KJV)

There are some things that will not make sense; however, God will allow them to bring glory through you. Decree today that God will get the glory in all that I have to endure on today; and all things will work together for my good in Jesus' Name. Those things that make no sense with no apparent explanation – God can use those things to show forth His glory in your life. God will cause all things to work together for your good, because you love Him and are called according to His purpose. Keep the faith. God is not asleep at the wheel but will give His angels charge over you to keep you so that you do not dash your feet against the stone. Enjoy His presence.

Daily Prayer

Father God, I pray that all I do today will bring glory to you, in the Name of Jesus, Amen.

THE LORD'S GOODNESS

"For the Lord is great, and greatly to be praised: He is to be feared above all gods. For all the gods of the nations are idols: but the Lord made the heavens."

Psalms 96:4-5 (KJV)

The Lord is good, His mercy is everlasting, and His truth endureth unto all generations. He is just good all the time! In bad times, God is still good. In sorrow, He is a comforter. In sad times, He is unspeakable joy. In confusion, He is peace that surpasses all understanding. When you can't find your way, He is the lamp unto your feet and a light unto your path. When lonely, He is a friend who will stick closer than a brother. When in need, He will supply all according to His riches in glory by Christ Jesus, Amen. Come what may, declare as Job did: "I would seek unto God, and unto God would I commit my cause: which doeth great things and unsearchable; marvelous things without number." God is just good, good all the time.

Daily Prayer

Father God, thank you for being so good to me in spite of what I may go through, in Jesus' Name.

DIVINE PLANS

"For which of you, intending to build a tower, sitteth not down first, and counteth the cost, whether he have sufficient to finish it?"

Luke 14:28 (KJV)

Before doing anything, commit it unto the Lord, for the Psalmist declared: "Commit thy way unto the Lord; trust also in Him; and He shall bring it to pass." Plans without actions equals frustration. Visions without provisions equals disappointments! Intentions without efforts equals nothing but wishing! It's not what you want but what you put efforts to that will cause you to be successful. No matter how small, the beginning is greater than what you will want or plan to do. If your efforts do not exceed your desires, frustrations will most likely be the outcome. Yes, commit your plans and desires unto the Lord, and He has promised to bring them to pass.

Daily Prayer

Father God, help me to never attempt to do anything before committing it to you first, in Jesus' Name, Amen.

FAITH THAT PLEASES GOD

"Through faith we understand that the worlds were framed by the word of God, so that things which ae seen were not made of things which do appear."
Hebrews 11:3 (KJV)

Without faith, it is impossible to please God. It is not a spare tire; it's not an after-all-else-fails strategy; it's not I-will-try-it-now last effort, but it's the real deal. Faith is the substance of things hoped for and the evidence of things not yet seen. It is what makes you act, move, or go after something that you want. It's not an afterthought, but it is the first thing that must be present before doing anything. Don't try anything without it. Yes, faith will move mountains, make all things possible, and cause you to see things that are not as if they were already done. Remember, without works, it is no good; put it to work for you today. Mustard seed faith will do.

Daily Prayer

Father God, please help me to walk in faith even when I don't see any results, in Jesus' Name, Amen.

WORLDLY LOVE

"Love not the world, neither the things that are in the world. If any man love the world, the love of the Father is not in him."

1 John 2:15 (KJV)

The love of the world is the enemy of the Lord. What is the love of the world? John declared the following: "for all that is in the world, the lust of the flesh, and the lust of the eyes, and the pride of life, is not of the Father, but is of the world." Why not love the world? Because each will cause you to be at odds with what the kingdom of God teaches. The closer you get to the Father, the further away you get from those things and people who do not fit into your future. The enemy will do all that he can to get you to follow the dictates of your flesh instead of following the leading of the Holy Spirit. Always remember that they that are in the flesh cannot please God. Be prayerful today.

Daily Prayer

Father God, help me to present my body as a living sacrifice, holy and acceptable unto you today, in Jesus' Name, Amen.

THE FAITHFUL GOD

"And being fully persuaded that, what He had promised, He was able also to perform."

Romans 4:21 (KJV)

Know for a certainty today that no matter what you need, God is able to perform it. There is nothing that is too difficult for the Lord to make happen on your behalf today. The only way the enemy can win is for you to quit, stop, give up, give in, give out, or abandon the call or position. But, since God is the power, energy, will, and reason behind the call; quitting, stopping, giving up, giving out, or abandoning the call are not options, "for it is God that works in you both to will and to do of His good pleasure." Be like Abraham. He was fully convinced that God was able to do what seemed impossible, and because of this strong conviction, he received what he asked for. Follow this example today.

Daily Prayer

Father God, thank you for being my strong tower that I can run to and find safety, in Jesus' Name, Amen.

WORTHY OF PRAISE

"Praise Him for His mighty acts: praise Him according to His excellent greatness."

Psalms 150:2 (KJV)

Let everything that hath breath praise the Lord. Praise is comely among the saints. When you praise, it's an invitation for the Lord to come and inherit your praises. The Psalmist declared: "Let the people praise thee, O God; let all the people praise thee. Then shall the earth yield her increase; and God, even our own God, shall bless us." This is what happens when you praise the Lord. Every morning is a day in which the Lord is worthy of all of your praise. Through praise, God delivered the enemy into the hands of His people, and it is a testimony to what He can do for us. All they did was sing and praise God. Then the Lord made the enemies turn and fight each other. Praise Him on purpose today.

Daily Prayer

Father God, I praise you for your mighty acts, your unconditional love, and for giving me all that I need to survive, in the Name of Jesus, Amen.

HOLY GUIDANCE

"For thou art my rock and my fortress; therefore for thy Name's sake lead me, and guide me."

Psalms 31:3 (KJV)

The Holy Spirit is a comforter, guide, and leader sent along to help you every day. Your day may not go as "you" have planned, but if you allow God, through the Holy Spirit, to direct you throughout the day, you will be able to make it through the day. He knows where to place every one of your steps! Be grateful for God's favor that is surrounding you, lifting you, covering you, keeping you, directing you, and putting people into your life who make serving in the Kingdom a joy! Know that what God has determined for you today will happen when God chooses, how He chooses, and where He chooses to make it happen. All we need to do is stay in His will. Today is a great opportunity to allow the Holy Spirit to lead you in His purpose.

Daily Prayer

Father God, please allow your Holy Spirit to lead and guide me throughout the day to fulfill all that you would have me to do, in Jesus' Name, Amen.

GRATITUDE

"Giving thanks always for all things unto God and the Father in the Name of our Lord Jesus Christ."

Ephesians 5:20 (KJV)

Disappointments may come, but there's encouragement in the Word of God. If you are hurting a bit today, know that there is a balm in Gilead. If you find yourself feeling a bit down, know that Christ is a lifter up of bowed down heads. If you have a great need on today, know that He is JEHOVAH JIREH (The Lord Will Provide). Don't allow yesterday's misfortunes to determine what you will try today. Whether it seems like it or not, know that God is working on your behalf today. Be thankful today for all that God is doing and will do on your behalf. Join in with what the Psalmist declared: "O give thanks unto the Lord, for He is good: for His mercy endureth forever." The Lord is good.

Daily Prayer

Father God, I thank you for being so good for me and for always making a way for me, in Jesus' Name, Amen.

HE WILL DELIVER

"He delivereth me from mine enemies: yea, thou liftest me up above those that rise up against me: thou hast delivered me from the violent man."
                                        Psalms 18:48 (KJV)

God will deliver you on time based upon His purpose for you each day. God has a set time, yes, a set time to deliver you. The Psalmist confirmed this by stating: "Thou shalt arise, and have mercy upon Zion: for the time to favour her, yea, the set time, is come." He further stated: "And the Lord shall help them, and deliver them: He shall deliver them from the wicked, and save them, because they trust in Him. No matter the issue, hold on to the promise! The Lord Himself stated: "And call upon Me in the day of trouble: I will deliver thee, and thou shalt glorify me." Fear not, the day of your deliverance is not nor will it be in question.

Daily Prayer

Father God, thank you for being my deliverer in times of trouble and for being the source of all my needs and protection, in Jesus' Name, Amen.

OUR REFUGE

"Trust in Him at all times; ye people, pour out your heart before Him: God is a refuge for us."

Psalms 62:8 (KJV)

God is a present help in time of trouble; He is a refuge for all who would seek comfort and peace in Him. In fact, "He is a refuge for the oppressed, a refuge in times of trouble." Refuge can be defined as "a condition of being safe or sheltered from pursuit, danger, or trouble." God fits all of these – and some. Solomon declared: "The Name of the Lord is a strong tower: the righteous runneth into it, and is safe." The Psalmist declared: "But I will sing of thy power; yea, I will sing aloud of thy mercy in the morning: for thou hast been my defence and refuge in the day of my trouble." You can rest in knowing today that God is your refuge from all foes.

Daily Prayer

Father God, thank you for being my refuge from the storms of life, a safe place where I can always turn for help, in Jesus' Name, Amen.

NOT HELPLESS

"He delivered me from my strong enemy, and from them which hated me: for they were too strong for me."

Psalms 18:17 (KJV)

Regardless of the situation or circumstance, you are not helpless. You are not nor will you be left to go at it alone today, no matter the situation. David declared: "By this I know that thou favourest me, because mine enemy doth not triumph over me." You are stronger that the enemy thinks and in most cases, stronger than you even think! The battle may be difficult, but as a believer, you have the "Greater Than" on your side. Moreover, any battle that God allows to confront you is a "fixed fight," and that's fixed in your favor. Believe that you will survive "this," God willing, regardless of what the enemy does or what the circumstance may be. You are not helpless in your battles.

Daily Prayer

Father God, thank you for delivering me from all my fears and the attacks of all my foes, in Jesus' Name, Amen.

TRIUMPHANT

"By this I know that thou favourest me, because mine enemy doth not tri-umph over me."

Psalms 41:11 (KJV)

You can be assured today that God is not asleep at the wheels in your life. He is watching over you, caring for you, providing for you, and defending you throughout the day. In fact, you are being kept by His mercy, loved unconditionally, saved by His Grace, and given all of these without reservations. You can be assured that your enemy will not triumph over you today, for Isaiah reminded us that "No weapon that is formed against us will prosper, and every tongue that rises up against us in judgement we shall condemn." The Lord will not give you over to the will of your enemy; not today, not ever.

Daily Prayer

Father God, thank you for always causing me to triumph over my enemies and not giving over to their will, in Jesus' Name, Amen.

SOLID FOUNDATION

"Thou hast enlarged my steps under me, that my feet did not slip."
Psalms 18:36 (KJV)

It is through Christ, the Holy Scripture, and the Holy Spirit that your foundation is established. The Scripture declared: "The steps of a good man are ordered by the Lord: and he delighteth in his way." King David declared: "He brought me up also out of an horrible pit, out of the miry clay, and set my feet upon a rock, and established by goings." If we follow the leading of the Holy Spirit, we are promised to get to our ordained destination. Solomon declared: "Trust in the Lord with all of thine heart; and lean not unto thine own understanding. In all thy ways acknowledge Him, and He shall direct thy paths." You are on a firm foundation with the Lord.

Daily Prayer

Father God, please lead me today, and every day, in the direction in which you would have me to go, in the Name of Jesus', Amen.

THE SOUND OF GOD

"Blessed is the people that know the joyful sound: they shall walk, O Lord, in the light of thy countenance."

Psalms 89:15 (KJV)

You awaken this morning to brand new mercies; regardless of the issues of yesterday, today you have new mercies. If you will seek to hear the voice of The Lord and follow the leading of the Holy Spirit, the Psalmist declared the following: "Happy are those who hear the joyful call to worship, for they will walk in the light of your presence, Lord. They rejoice all day long in your wonderful reputation. They exult in your righteousness." What a wonderful position to take and what a wonderful honor from knowing and hearing the joyful sounds of worship toward the Lord. Jesus stated: "My sheep know my voice, and a stranger they will not follow." Know Him.

Daily Prayer

Father God, please help me to listen to and adhere to the sound of your voice, not just today but every day, in Jesus' Name, Amen.

NOT ASHAMED

"O keep my soul, and deliver me: let me not be ashamed; for I put my trust in thee."

Psalms 25:20 (KJV)

It is not the Lord's will for any of His children to walk in shame but in honor and the glory that He has designed for them. In fact, the Psalmist declared: "The Lord knoweth the days of the upright: and their inheritance shall be forever. They shall not be ashamed in the evil time: and in the days of famine they shall be satisfied." You are an overcomer; you are more than a conqueror; you are fearfully and wonderfully made; you are blessed and highly favored; you are made in the image and likeness of God; you are loved unconditionally. You are the apple of God's eye and His workmanship created for good works. Because of these things, and by walking in the ways of the Kingdom, you will not be put to shame. Rejoice in the Lord today.

Daily Prayer

Father God, thank you for being my provider and protector and for not allowing me to be put to shame at the hands of my enemies, in Jesus' Name, Amen.

GOD'S GREATNESS

"Thy righteousness also, O God, is very high, who hast done great things: O God, who is like unto thee!"

Psalms 71:19 (KJV)

Great is the Lord and greatly to be praised. The Book of 2 Samuel declared: "Wherefore thou art great, O Lord God: for there is none like thee, neither is there any God besides thee, according to all that we have heard with our ears." He further stated: "For who is God, save the Lord? And who is a rock, save our God?" "Great is the Lord, and greatly to b praised: He also is to be feared above all gods." Apostle Paul declared in the Book of Ephesians: "Now unto Him that is able to do exceeding abundantly above all that we can ask or think, according to the power that worketh in us." Yes, our God is great, and there is nothing too difficult for Him. Call on him today to meet all your needs.

Daily Prayer

Father God, I praise you for your goodness and your mighty acts in my life, in Jesus' Name, Amen.

STAY CONNECTED

"If ye abide in me, and my words abide in you, ye shall ask what ye will, and it shall be done unto you."

John 15:7 (KJV)

It is the Word of God that keeps us connected to the Father, His will, His plan, and His purpose for our lives. Without it, we are not able to withstand the schemes, attacks, or distractions of the enemy. Jesus declared: "Abide in Me, and I in you. As the branch cannot bear fruit of itself, except it abide in the vine; no more can ye, except ye abide in me. I am the vine, ye are the branches: He that abideth in me, and I in him, the same bringeth forth much fruit: for without Me ye can do nothing." All our strength is in Him, and if we stay connected to Him – the Source – we will receive all that He has intended for us to receive. Don't go anywhere without this connection.

Daily Prayer

Father God, help me to remain attached to the vine so that I can receive all that you have for me, in the Name of Jesus, Amen.

THE WATCHFUL EYE

"Behold, the eye of the Lord is upon them that fear Him, upon them that hope in His mercy."

Psalms 33:18 (KJV)

Y ou are never out of the sight of the Lord God nor are you ever not under His divine protection. The Psalmist declared: "Because thou hast made the Lord, which is my refuge even the most High, thy habitation; There shall no evil befall thee, neither shall any plague come nigh thy dwelling. For He shall give His angels charge over thee, to keep thee in all thy ways. They shall bear thee up in their hands, lest thou dash thy foot against a stone." He will never forsake nor leave you, and His presence will be a shelter for you, regardless of what confronts you on today. Rest assured that God is watching over you to perform all His plans for you on today. Enjoy this presence.

Daily Prayer

Father God, thank you for watching over me and leading, guiding, providing, and protecting me throughout the day, in Jesus' Name, Amen.

LIFE IN THE SEED

"And sow the fields, and plant vineyards, which may yield fruits of increase."
Psalms 107:37 (KJV)

Whatever you do today is really a seed into your future, knowing that the seed that leaves your hands can affect your future, good or bad. The Book of Ecclesiastes declared: "As thou knowest not what is the way of the spirit, nor how the bones do grow in the womb of her that is with child: even so thou knowest not the works of God who maketh all. In the morning sow thy seed, and in the evening withhold not thine hand; for thou knowest not whether shall prosper, either this or that, or whether they both shall be alike good." The Lord has given us seedtime and harvest for our benefit, and they will never cease. Sow something today into your future.

Daily Prayer

Father God, show me where and into whom to sow today that my harvest will be according to Thy will, in Jesus' Name, Amen.

IF YOU SEARCH

"I sought the Lord, and He heard me, and delivered me from all my fears."
Psalms 34:4 (KJV)

If you go after God, you will find His compassion, love, mercy, grace, power, and provisions. The Prophet Jeremiah was inspired to write: "And ye shall seek me, and find me, when ye shall search for me with all your heart. And I will be found of you, saith the Lord: and I will turn away your captivity and I will gather you from all the nations, and from all the places whither I have driven you, saith the Lord; and I will bring you again into the place whence I caused you to be carried away captive." Seek His will; seek His plan; seek His purpose; seek His ways that you may prosper in the things that He has or will make available to you. Seek Him. He's waiting for you to come to Him.

Daily Prayer

Father God, please help me to fully commit all my ways to you so that I do not stumble along my way, in Jesus' Name, Amen.

MY ALL AND ALL

"In God is my salvation and my glory: the rock of my strength, and my refuge, is in God."

Psalms 62:7

Your day begins and ends with Christ, for it is in Him that you move, live, and exist. With Him, you can do all that He strengthens you to do, but without Him you cannot do anything. King David declared: "For thou art my lamp, O Lord: and the Lord will lighten my darkness. For by thee I have run through a troop: by my God have I leaped over a wall." Isaiah declared: "For the Lord God will help me; therefore, shall I not be confounded: therefore have I set my face like a flint, and I know that I shall not be ashamed." Yes, God is your salvation and your glory: the rock of your strength, your refuge, and always a present help in the time of trouble. Enjoy.

Daily Prayer

Father God, thank you for being my all and all, regardless of what I may find myself faced with, in the Name of Jesus', Amen.

BECAUSE OF GRACE

"But by the grace of God I am what I am: and His grace which was bestowed upon me was not in vain; but I labored more abundantly than they all: yet not I, but the grace of God which was with me."

1 Corinthians 15:10 (KJV)

It is by and through God's amazing grace that you are able to move about during the day. Apostle Paul declared that God's grace is sufficient for all that you will encounter on today. You were saved by grace, kept by grace, empowered by grace, and it is through grace that you are able to do all that God has ordained you to do. The Psalmist stated: "For the Lord God is a sun and shield: the Lord will give grace and glory: no good thing will He withhold from them that walk uprightly." You can be assured today that this grace does not need an invitation to operate on your behalf. It is provided to you because of the unconditional love of God.

Daily Prayer

Father God, thank you for your grace that keeps me through all that I encounter, in the Name of Jesus, Amen.

DIVINE GIFTS

"Wherefore He saith, When He ascended up on high, He led captivity captive, and gave gifts unto men."

Ephesians 4:8 (KJV)

God has given you your awesome gifts and talents, and you should be sure that you try to use all of them for the Kingdom, your family, your community, and all that God directs you to do. You have been gifted to be a blessing to others and for the furtherance of the Kingdom. God does not regret the gifts He has given you, so be sure to use them to the glory of God. No need to compare yourself to anyone else. God has made you unique for what He has called you to do. You can be assured that it is "God that works in you both to will and to do of His good pleasure." You are a gift; be a blessing to someone today.

Daily Prayer

Father God, thank you for gifting me to do what you have ordained me to do. I know it is only in what you have empowered me to do that I can succeed, in the Name of Jesus, Amen.

PEACEFUL MOMENTS

"Now the Lord of peace Himself give you peace always by all means. The Lord be with you all."

2 Thessalonians 3:16 (KJV)

The peace that God has for you today surpasses all understanding. It is not as the world gives but only as the Lord can give because He is the God of peace. Jesus said in the Gospel of John: "Peace I leave with you, my peace I give unto you: not as the world giveth, give I unto you. Let not your heart be troubled, neither let it be afraid." This is not a temporary peace, a fading peace, or a conditional peace. The Prophet Isaiah declared: "Thou wilt keep him in perfect peace, whose mind is stayed on thee: because he trusteth in thee." Today, "Let the peace of God rule in your heart" through the Holy Spirit, in the Name of Jesus.

Daily Prayer

Father God, thank you for giving me your peace that surpasses all understanding today, in the Name of Jesus, Amen.

DIVINE CALLING

"Let every man abide in the same calling wherein he was called."
1 Corinthians 7:20 (KJV)

Always remember that God's gifts and callings are without repentance, meaning that God does not regret giving you what you possess. It is the Lord who called you, gifted you, equipped you, and enabled you to do what you are currently doing and will do in the future. You do not have to be well known to do great things. Be great right where you are. In the words of Dr. King: "If I cannot do great things, I can do small things in a great way." Stay true to your calling, dream, and vision no matter who stops believing in you. You have been given your gifts and your calling by God, and He will never give up on what He has placed inside of you. Praise Him today for your awesome gift and for the calling He has placed on your life.

Daily Prayer

Father God, thank you for using me today to help others as directed by your Spirit, in Jesus' Name, Amen.

THE LORD'S DOING

"For whether we live, we live unto the Lord; and whether we die, we die unto the Lord: whether we live therefore, or die, we are the Lord's."

Romans 14:8 (KJV)

Your life is because of and through Christ. Everything is because of Him. It is He who works in you both to will and to do of His good pleasure. If you succeed, it is because of Christ. It you move, it is because of Christ. Regardless of your achievements, it is all because Christ, through the Holy Spirit, enabled you to do it. James declared: "Every good gift and every perfect give is from above, and cometh down from the Father of lights, with whom is no variableness, neither shadow of turning. Of His own will begat He us with the Word of truth, that we should be a kind of first fruits of His righteousness." Yes, it's the Lord's doing and it is marvelous in our sight.

Daily Prayer

Father God, thank you for always being more than enough for me and for always meeting my needs, in the Name of Jesus, Amen.

BY THE WORD

"In the beginning was the Word, and the Word was with God, and the Word was God."

John 1:1 (KJV)

The Word is responsible for all creation and is responsible for holding all things together in the world. It declares: "All things were made by Him; and without Him was not anything made that was made. In Him was life; and the life was the light of men." The Hebrews writer declared this about Christ (The Word): "Who being the brightness of His glory, and he express image of His person, and upholding all things by the word of His power, when He had by Himself purged our sins, sat down on the right hand of Majesty on high." The Word: you are kept, directed, protected, and promoted by the power of the Word. Allow it to keep the enemy at bay, to be your encouragement and a light unto your path.

Daily Prayer

Father God, thank you for your Word; thank you allowing me to experience your presence through your Word every day, in Jesus' Name, Amen.

A NEW THING

"Behold, I will do a new thing; now it shall spring forth; shall ye not know it? I will even make a way in the wilderness, and rivers in the desert."

Isaiah 43:19 (KJV)

As you begin your new day, decree that the Lord will perfect all that concerns me. If you follow the leading of Holy Spirit, nothing will be left undone for you today. God knows when, where, and how to make all things work together for your good, regardless of your past mistakes, missteps, or current situation or circumstance. The Word of God instructs us to "Trust in the Lord with all of thine heart, and lean not unto your own understanding. In all of your ways acknowledge God, and He will direct your path." You were afforded new mercies this morning, and this day was not given to you with yesterday in mind, but for new opportunities, new blessings, and decisions. Yes, this is your new beginning.

Daily Prayer

Father God, thank you for my new day, one filled with new mercies, in Jesus' Name, Amen.

SURE PURPOSE

"For the Lord of hosts hath purposed, and who shall disannul it? And His hand is stretched out, and who shall turn it back?"

Isaiah 14:27 (KJV)

God determines the time and season to bless and favor us. Nothing can stop or impede these promises and provisions from coming to pass. If God is for you, there is no need to worry about who or what is against you. It is through Christ that you live, move, and have your very existence. It is God who works in you both to will and to do of His good pleasure. Nothing can prevent God from causing His favor from being upon you, causing every good and perfect gift to come upon you. What God has purposed for you cannot be undone by the will, desire, or intentions of man. All we need to do is to abide in Him and allow His Word to abide in us; then we can ask whatever we want, and it will be given unto us. That's His promise; receive it today

Daily Prayer

Father God, please help me to walk in my purpose and to do all that I can in respect to the purpose that you have for me on today, in Jesus' Name, Amen.

GOD'S GIFT

"For the law was given by Moses, but grace and truth came by Jesus Christ."
John 1:17 (KJV)

God's gift of grace has been defined by some as "God's riches at Christ's expense." This amazing gift is given to us because of God's unconditional love for us through Christ Jesus. This gift does not need an invitation to show up; it will be available to you today, on time, in time, and every time. Nothing you will encounter today will be greater than the Grace of God. Nothing you will have to do today is more powerful than the benefits that Grace will offer you on today. Grace will see the need and supply it; He will see your struggle and come to your rescue; He will keep an eye on you all day long, being all that you need Him to be. Why is this? Because Christ is the Grace of God. Enjoy and embrace this grace in its fullness today.

Daily Prayer

Father God, thank you for wrapping me in your amazing Grace all day, keeping me, leading me, and caring for me, in Jesus' Name, Amen.

GODLY PROTECTION

"Don't be afraid, for I am with you. Don't be discouraged, for I am your God. I will strengthen you and help you. I will hold you up with my victorious right hand."

Isaiah 41:10 (NLT)

Regardless of what you encounter on today – no matter what the enemy throws at you – your help, your source, your provision, your protection will remain the same. God is and will always be more than enough, no matter what you encounter. Rest assured that God is the same yesterday, today, and forever. Declare today as the Psalmist did: "I will lift up mine eyes unto the hills, from whence cometh my help. My help cometh from the Lord, which made heaven and earth. He will not suffer thy foot to be moved: He that keepeth thee will not slumber nor sleep." God is always a present help, and no one or nothing can pluck you out of His hands. Enjoy your day; nothing can sneak up on Him.

Daily Prayer

Father God, I trust you today for all of my needs, protection, and guidance, in Jesus' name, Amen.

GODLY DELIVERANCE

"They cried unto thee, and were delivered: they trusted in thee, and were not confounded."

Psalms 22:5 (KJV)

God is forever faithful to you, to His word, to His promise, to His purpose. Even when we are faithless, He is faithful. The Psalmist declared: "Then they cried unto the Lord in their trouble, and He delivered them out of their distresses." King David gave an assuring testimony to the delivering power of our Lord God when he stated: "But thou, O Lord, art a shield for me; my glory, and the lifter up of mine head. I cried unto the Lord with my voice, and He heard me out of His holy hill... I laid me down and slept; I awaked; for the Lord sustained me. I will not be afraid of ten thousands of people, that have set themselves against me round about." He will deliver you.

Daily Prayer

Father God, thank you for your deliverance, now and in the future, in the Name of Jesus, Amen.

DIVINE SECURITY

"The Lord is my light and my salvation; whom shall I fear? The Lord is the strength of my life; of whom shall I be afraid?"

Psalms 27:1 (KJV))

Thank God our lives are not at the mercy of man or the devices of the enemy. What some call defeats, God will use them to mature and promote you. The unfairness of life cannot compete or be compared with the unconditional love, amazing grace, and favor of our merciful God. What is meant to be, by and through Him, will come into our lives – period! There is no need to fear or walk in anxiety. God is for you, and since He is, who can be against you? He is greater than any enemy, bigger that any obstacle, and more powerful than any force that you will face today or in the future. Trust the leading of the Holy Spirit, and you will outlast the attacks of the enemy.

Daily Prayer

Father God, thank you for being my source for all that I need and my light for dark days, in the Name of Jesus, Amen.

CLEAR VISION

"For the vision is yet for an appointed time, but at the end it shall speak, and not lie: though it tarry, wait for it; because it will surely come, it will not tarry."

Habakkuk 2:3 (KJV)

If your dream or vision is really important to you, stick with it like a postage stamp. The stamp stays with the package until it gets to the intended destination. Even if a package or letter goes to the wrong address, the same stamp will get the package to the right one if it's put back in the mail. If your dream or vision is God-given, stick with it until it comes to pass. Never get tired of doing what is right, what you have been called to do, what you believe is your God-given call to do. Don't get weary in well-doing, for you will reap if you don't give up and stop. Your vision is for an appointed time, and it will come to pass on schedule, His schedule. Trust Him.

Daily Prayer

Father God, please help me to stay in line with your plan for me on today, and don't allow me to stray from the vision you have given me, in the Name of Jesus, Amen.

BY YOUR FRUIT

"Ye shall know them by their fruits. Do men gather grapes of thorns, or figs of thistles?"

Matthew 7:16 (KJV)

Every tree is known by the fruit it produces. Only orange trees produce oranges; only pear trees produce pears. If you want to know what kind of tree it is, simply inspect the fruit. Our lives are no different. We are known by the fruit that our lives produce. As believers, we are expected to produce fruit that is pleasing unto the Father. The Gospel according to Matthew declared: "Either make the tree good, and his fruit good; or else make the tree corrupt, and his fruit corrupt: for the tree is known by the fruit it bears." Today is a great day for your fruit to be made known and pleasing unto the Lord. John declared: "Here is the Father glorified, that ye bear much fruit, so shall ye be my disciples."

Daily Prayer

Father God, help me to produce fruit that will be pleasing unto you on today, in the Name of Jesus, Amen.

GOD'S WAY

"But God hath chosen the foolish things of the world to confound the wise; and God hath chosen the weak things of the world to confound the things which are mighty."

1 Corinthians 1:27 (KJV)

Do not allow what may not make sense to anyone else stop you from pursuing that same thing. Follow your God-given dream or vision, no matter what the distractors or naysayers might say. It's your vision or dream, and the thoughts and opinions of others can be considered; however, they should not determine what you should do about what God has given you. Know for certain that if it was meant for them, they would pursue it was well. God knows how to keep you from falling; He knows how to direct your path; He knows how to make your enemies your footstool. God will do what He has promised. Today has a plan and purpose; following the leading of the Holy Spirit will allow them to be fulfilled in you.

Daily Prayer

Father God, thank you for allowing me the opportunity to experience your awesome presence on every level today, in the Name of Jesus' Amen.

GODLY SECURITY

"When thou liest down, thou shalt not be afraid: yea, thou shalt lie down, and thy sleep shall be sweet."

Proverbs 3:24 (KJV)

You can rest assured that you are never out of His sight, never too low that He cannot reach you, never too high that He cannot humble you, never too needy that He cannot supply your every need. Nothing can separate us from the love of God, and He takes pleasure in the prosperity of His people. The favor of God and he Grace of God are always available to you, regardless of the situation or circumstance in which you may find yourself. You are always on the mind of God and never too anything that He cannot not come to your rescue. You can declare as the Psalmist did: "Thou art my hiding place; thou shalt preserve me from trouble, thou shalt compass me about with songs of deliverance." Christ is your unmoving security at all times.

Daily Prayer

Father God, thank you for being my security no matter what I am facing, in the Name of Jesus, Amen.

DIVINE PROMOTION

"But God is the Judge: He putteth down one, and setteth up another."
Psalms 75:7 (KJV)

Regardless of the situation or circumstance, God is responsible for your promotion. Please know that promotion is by God, through God, and because of God. It does not depend upon the will, wishes, or approval of man! The Psalmist declared: "For promotion cometh neither from the east nor from the west, nor from the south. But God is the judge: He putteth down one, and setteth up another." When it's God's will to promote you, He can change the times and the seasons to make it happen. Know that every good and perfect gift comes from above (God), every one of them. Man cannot determine when, how, and from where your promotion comes. God has a set time to bless you; and when that time comes, no enemy has the power to change it or stop it.

Daily Prayer

Father God, thank you for being responsible for when, where, and how I am promoted, in the Name of Jesus, Amen.

TRUTH IN THE WORD

"For the Word of the Lord is right; and all His works are done in truth."

Psalms 33:4 (KJV)

The truth may not make you feel good, but it will certainly free you! A half-truth is a whole lie. As a believer, it is not what you accept as truth but what God has said is true. And, "ye shall know the truth, and the truth shall make you free." Don't allow what others think distract you from known truth. Again, it may not make you feel good, be happy, or seem right, but you will be free. The Word of God is true; it has been tried and proven to be true. You do not have to try to modify it or alter it. The truth has and will continue to stand the test of time. With this in mind, you can know that whatsoever God has said about you, to you, and for you will surely come to pass. Trust this truth for all you need today.

Daily Prayer

Father God, thank you for your Word that brings truth to my life, in the Name of Jesus, Amen.

WHY SHOULD I FEAR

"The Lord is on my side; I will not fear: what can man do unto me?"
Psalms 118:6 (KJV)

Regardless of who is against you, who hates you, or who fights you, remember, the Lord is on your side. Thank God that the opinions of others do not change how or what God thinks about you. If God be for you, and He certainly is, who or what can be against you? God's favor towards you does not see, hear, or recognize the will or wishes of others. In fact, what the enemy thought would take you out, God used to lift you up, for "Greater is He that is in you than he that is in the world." Declare as the Psalmist: "When the wicked, even mine enemies and my foes, came upon me to eat up my flesh, they stumbled and fell." It's your testimony.

Daily Prayer

Father God, thank you again and again for being my shield and protector against all of my foes, in the Name of Jesus, Amen.

ALL SPIRITUAL BLESSINGS

"Blessed be the God and Father of our Lord Jesus Christ, who hath blessed us with all spiritual blessings in heavenly places in Christ."

Ephesians 1:3 (KJV)

God has made every spiritual blessing in heaven available to you, now, here on earth. Nothing that heaven has prepared for you to have here on earth has been or will be withheld from you. God's unconditional love, His access to the throne, and His Holy Spirit are all available to you each day, waiting to assist you in every area of your life. The Word reminds us that "we can come boldly to the throne of grace, that we may obtain mercy, and find grace to help in time of need." And for comfort, Jesus declared in the Gospel of John: "And I will pray the Father, and He shall give you another Comforter, that He may abide with you forever." God has made His heavenly blessings available to you without measure; embrace them now!

Daily Prayer

Father God, I pray your kingdom come, Thy Will be done, in earth as it is in heaven, in the Name of Jesus, Amen.

GODLY BENEFITS

"Blessed be the Lord, who daily loadeth us with benefits, even the God of our salvation."

Psalms 68:19 (KJV)

Celebrate today; it is a gift. Don't be afraid of what the enemy tries to do or what you may face on today. It all has to pass the Lord's desk before it gets to you. God knows exactly how much you can handle. This is the day that the Lord has made, rejoice and be glad in it. Apostle Paul declared: "For ye know the grace of our Lord Jesus Christ, that, though He was rich, yet for your sakes He became poor, that ye through His poverty might be rich." Yes, He loads us with blessings and benefits every day. His mercies are new to and for you every day. These are for you without the need to pray for them. The Father knows what you have need of before you ask. Rejoice and be glad today. God will never run out of the grace or mercies that you may need.

Daily Prayer

Father God, thank you for blessing me beyond measure today, in the Name of Jesus, Amen.

FIGHTING FOR YOU

"For the Lord you God is He that goeth with you, to fight for you against your enemies, to save you."

Deuteronomy 20:4 (KJV)

There is no victory without a battle, no testimony without a test, no winner without a contest. Every victory comes after the struggle, which produces a testimony. Be mindful of what the scripture said: "They overcame him by the blood of the Lamb, and by the word of their testimony; and they loved not their lives unto the death." If there is to be a victory, there has to be a war; if you will be an overcomer, you must overcome something that opposes you. However, always engage in battle knowing that "no weapon that is formed against you will prosper." God is on your side, which makes you more than a conqueror throughout the day.

Daily Prayer

Father God, thank you for fighting for me, always abiding with me, protecting me, in the Name of Jesus, Amen.

IN TOTAL CONFIDENCE

"For the Lord shall be thy confidence, and shall keep thy foot from being taken."

Proverbs 3:26 (KJV)

You can rest assured today that God will keep you, regardless of the situation, condition, or circumstance. When there are things that just do not make any sense and you can't understand why or how, trust God to see and carry you through them. The Book of Jude declared: "Now unto Him that is able to keep you from falling, and to present you faultless before the presence of His glory with exceeding joy, to the only wise God our Savior, be glory and majesty, dominion and power, both now and ever. Amen." You can rest assured that God is able to keep you, protect you, lead you, and provide for you throughout the day. Trust Him.

Daily Prayer

Father God, thank you for being my source for all my needs and for leading me throughout the day, in Jesus' Name, Amen.

NO OTHER BUT GOD

"Remember the former things of old: for I am God, and there is none else; I am God, and there is none like me."

Isaiah 46:9 (KJV)

Praise God! He is Alpha and Omega, the Beginning and the End, the First and the Last. He knows all things, can do all things, and is everywhere at the same time. Yes, He is all-knowing, all-seeing, and all-powerful. You do not have to beg for provisions; He provides them freely. You do not have to worry about protection, for He is a strong tower; the righteous run to Him and are safe. There is nothing too difficult for God; "He is able to do exceeding abundantly above all that you can ask or think according to the power that works within you." He is King of kings and Lord of lords, and He is on your side; why fear what man can do unto you?

Daily Prayer

Father God, thank you for being my source in time of need, for I know that there is nothing too difficult for you to do, in Jesus' Name, Amen.

MY TOTAL SOURCE

"The God of my rock; in Him will I trust: He is my shield, and the horn of my salvation, my high tower, and my refuge, my savior; thou savest me from violence."

2 Samuel 22:3 (KJV)

Today, if you are feeling under attack from the enemy, know that God is your source, your foundation, your salvation, and safe place. Know that "When the enemy shall come in like a flood, the Spirit of the Lord will lift up a standard against him." He is your Rock; therefore, you can stand on a solid foundation. You can rest assured that He is watching over you, protecting you, and shielding you from what would do you harm throughout the day. The Lord spoke in the Book of Isaiah: "I, even I, am the Lord; and beside me there is no saviour." And, since He is for you, working on your behalf, who can be against you? Be certain today that the Lord God is on your side.

Daily Prayer

Father God, you are my Rock in whom I depend and trust, in the Name of Jesus, Amen

NEVER FORSAKEN

"For the Lord will not cast off His people, neither will He forsake His inheritance."

Psalms 94:14 (KJV)

You will never be forgotten or forsaken by the Lord. You are the apple of His eye, and no one is able to pluck you out of His hands. His love for thee is unconditional, and His mercy is everlasting. King David wrote a definitive statement concerning this when he wrote: "I have been young, and now am old; yet have I not seen the righteous forsaken, nor his seed begging bread." God is working on your behalf now, will be doing so on tomorrow, and has your future under control as well. He is not making it up as you go along, but He has a "plan to prosper you, and to bring you to an expected end." In fact, He has declared your end from the beginning. You will not be forsaken nor forgotten on today – not even for a second.

Daily Prayer

Father God, thank you for always keeping me in your divine care and for always making a way for me, in the Name of Jesus, Amen.

SATISFIED IN HIM

"With long life will I satisfy him, and shew him my salvation."
Psalms 91:16 (KJV)

Apostle John declared: "Beloved, I wish above all things that thou mayest prosper and be in health, even as thy soul prospereth." Yes, God wants to prosper you, bless you, and give you a long and prosperous life. God does all things well. Be excited about what's coming, for God will not do less that what He has already done for you. He is no respecter of persons; believe that what He has done for you in the past doesn't even remotely compare to what He will do for you in the future. Yes, God wants to satisfy you with a long good life; be sensitive to the leading of the Holy Spirt and watch what God will reveal to you on today. His favor is awesome.

Daily Prayer

Father God, I thank and praise you for all of the blessings that you have bestowed upon me, in Jesus' Name, Amen.

SEPARATED FOR HIM

"Wherefore come out from among them, and be ye separate, saith the Lord, and touch not the unclean thing; and I will receive you."

2 Corinthians 6:17 (KJV)

Being diligent with what you surrounding yourself will go far in your success each day. King David declared: "Blessed is the man that walketh not in the counsel of the ungodly, nor standeth in the way of sinners, nor sitteth in the seat of the scornful. But his delight is in the law of the Lord; and in His law doth he meditate day and night." Why is this so? Because two cannot walk together unless they agree. Reject what God rejects, accept what the Word has declared, and approve of what God has approved in the scripture. Trying to take people with you who are opposed to your values will result in aborted missions. Please know those who labor among you.

Daily Prayer

Father God, help me today to separate myself from all that would cause me to miss my assignment on today, in Jesus' Name, Amen.

DIVINE COVERING

"The Lord is on my side; I will not fear: what can man do unto me?"
Psalms 118:6 (KJV)

If God be for you, and He certainly is, who can really be against you?! We know that "Greater is He, God, that is in you than he that is in the world." Who or what can compete with this? There is really no need to fear, for the Greater Than lives on the inside of you. The Psalmist declared: "The Lord is my light and my salvation; whom shall I fear? The Lord is the strength of my life; of whom shall I be afraid? When the wicked, even mine enemies and my foes, came upon me to eat up my flesh, they stumbled and fell. Though an host should encamp against me, my heart shall not fear: though war should rise against me, in this will I be confident." The Lord is your confidence today.

Daily Prayer

Father God, thank you for being on my side and for being my strong tower from the storms of life, in the Name of Jesus, Amen.

FROM TEARS TO JOY

"They that sow in tears shall reap in joy."

Psalms 126:5 (KJV)

There may be times when it seems as if you are not making a difference or that your efforts are going unnoticed; but God has not forgotten you, has not overlooked you, and will not allow your good deeds to go unrewarded. Apostle Paul encouraged us not to grow "weary in well doing: for in due season, we shall reap if we faint not." You will reap a harvest; just keep doing what God has purposed you to do, regardless of the lack of support or recognition from man. You may have been sowing in tears lately, but the Word states that you will reap in joy. Remember, "weeping may endure for a night, but joy cometh in the morning." Keep sowing, it will pay off.

Daily Prayer

Father God, help me to remain diligent in my giving, even when I do not see the harvest that I need, in the Name of Jesus, Amen.

REWARD OF THE FAITHFUL

"O love the Lord, all ye His saints: for the Lord preserveth the faithful, and plentifully rewardeth the proud doer."

Psalms 31:23 (KJV)

According to the Word, "The faithful shall abound in blessings." The Psalmist declared: "The Lord preserveth the faithful, and plentifully rewardeth the proud doer." In other words, your faithfulness and work in the Kingdom will not go unrewarded. The Lord declared: "Be thou faithful unto death, and I will give thee a crown of life." When you are faithful in that which is least, God will reward you with greater responsibilities and duties. Christ declared in the Gospel of Matthew: "His lord said unto him, Well done thou good land faithful servant: thou hast been faithful over a few things, I will make thee ruler over many things: enter thou into the joy of the Lord."

Daily Prayer

Father God, thank you for always providing me with blessings and favor, in the Name of Jesus, Amen.

HIDING PLACE

"For in the time of trouble He shall hide me in His pavilion: in the secret of His tabernacle shall He hide me; He shall set me up upon a rock."

Psalms 27:5 (KJV)

The Name of the Lord is a strong tower: the righteous runneth into it and is safe." God will never forsake you in troubled times nor in times of distress. King David declared: "Many are the afflictions of the righteous, yet God does deliver them out of them all." When it feels like you are all alone, you've got to know that you are not alone. When you don't even feel His presence, you've got to believe He is there all the time. He is always a present help in the time of trouble. Don't be discouraged. At one time or another, these feelings try to attack everyone. But, what God has done for others, He will do for you. When you don't know what to do, trust Him to direct your next steps.

Daily Prayer

Father God, thank you for being my hiding place from every storm and for always being my resting place, in the Name of Jesus, Amen.

RENEWED

"Who satisfieth thy mouth with good things; so that thy youth is renewed like the eagle's."

Psalms 103:5 (KJV)

What you feed will grow, whether it's faith or doubt. "Death and life are in the power of the tongue, and a man's belly shall be satisfied with the fruit of his mouth, and with the increase of his lips shall he be filled." Speak life to any dormant situation in your life. Speak those things that be not as though they were already done. God will not give you anything that will be harmful to you or your walk with Him. "Every good and perfect gift comes from above," and it is God's will that you prosper and be in health even as your soul prospers. Yes, God wants to satisfy your mouth with good things; so that your youth is renewed as the eagle's. Enjoy the benefits.

Daily Prayer

Father God, thank you for being my continuous help and provider for all that I need, in Jesus' Name, Amen.

THE LORD; MY KEEPER

"The Lord is the portion of mine inheritance and of my cup: thou maintainest my lot."

Psalms 16:5 (KJV)

All that you have and all that you will ever obtain is because of the Lord. He is the Way, the Truth, and the Life. You are kept by Him, led by Him, and guided by Him. Jesus declared in the Gospel of John: "I am the vine, ye are the branches: He that abideth in me, and I in him, the same bringeth forth much fruit: for without Me ye can do nothing." The Psalmist declared: "For thou hast delivered my soul from death, mine eyes from tears, and my feet from falling." Isaiah declared: "For the Lord God will help me; therefore, shall I not be confounded: therefore, have I set my face like a flint, and I know that I shall not be ashamed." This is the Lord's doing – enjoy it.

Daily Prayer

Father God, you are my life, my way, and my hope; without you I am nothing, but I can do all things through Christ which strengthens me, in Jesus' Name, Amen.

LIFE AND FAVOR

"Thou hast granted me life and favour, and thy visitation hath preserved my spirit."

Job 10:12 (KJV)

It is through Christ that we live, move, and have our being. Through Christ, we can do all things, but without Him we can do nothing. God's favor will never run out. His mercy endures forever. His grace us unlimited. His love is unequal and unconditional. He has given you life and favor, which no one is able to take away from you. You can't get too low, move too far, or do anything that God's grace and love will not reach you. Nothing can separate you from the love of God through Christ Jesus. It is His pleasure to give you new life, and He does this by providing you new mercies every morning. His presence is preserving you, regardless of what you do or don't do each day.

Daily Prayer

Father God, thank you for giving me new mercies each morning so that I receive new life and favor each day, in the Name of Jesus, Amen.

CORRECTED TO GROW

"Every branch in me that beareth not fruit He taketh away: and every branch that beareth fruit, He purgeth it, that it may bring forth more fruit."
John 15:2 (KJV)

If every good and perfect gift comes from above, we can know then where the evil or bad ones come from. God may sometimes take away from us things or people to increase or improve us so that we may become even more productive. It is His will that we produce much fruit. To make sure that this happens, He takes away every branch that does not bear fruit; and every branch that does bear fruit, He prunes so that the branch can bring forth more fruit. All of your help comes from the Lord, regardless of how much you have or will accomplish. God wants you to always bear fruit and that this fruit remains. He chastens those whom He loves; the chastening or correcting is to grow you not to harm you. Let Him grow you today.

Daily Prayer

Father God, help me to withstand the needed corrections so that I may grow, in the Name of Jesus, Amen.

ALL POWER

"Great is our Lord, and of great power: His understanding is infinite."
Psalms 147:5 (KJV)

All power belongs unto the Lord God. His powers are unlimited, His knowledge is unlimited, His grace is sufficient, His mercy is everlasting, and His love is unconditional. There is no power that can be compared unto His, and nothing is too difficult for Him. Regardless of your need on today, He is able to do exceeding abundantly above all that you can ask or think. He is always more than enough and greater than any force, power, or situation that you may encounter on today. His greatness will always supersede your failures. This greatness is unmatched by any other, and He is on your side, so who can be against you? Enjoy His presence today.

Daily Prayer

Father God, thank you for your great power and for always being more than enough for me, regardless of what I will face, in the Name of Jesus, Amen.

BEYOND NATURAL SIGHT

"In the morning sow thy seed, and in the evening withhold not thine hand: for thou knowest not whether shall prosper, either this or that, or whether they both shall be alike good."

Ecclesiastes 11:6 (KJV)

Don't worry, conditions do have to be perfect for God to favor and prosper you. No matter what it looks like now, it's a perfect time for a breakthrough, a perfect time for a promotion, a perfect time for increase, a perfect time for a miracle. Imperfect surroundings or conditions are no match for a perfect God. There is no condition, situation, or circumstance that can prevent God from causing increase to come into your life. Nothing is too difficult for God: nothing too hard for Him to work out. God can cause a river to come to a desert, make a mountain a molehill, and turn water into wine. Don't allow the surroundings to dictate what you do next.

Daily Prayer

Father God, please help me to be open to the leading of the Holy Spirit on when and where to sow my seed, in the Name of Jesus, Amen.

IN GOD'S THOUGHTS

"How precious are thy thoughts unto me, O God! How great is the sum of them!"

Psalms 139:17 (KJV)

You are always on the mind of the Father. Yes, the Lord is thinking about you every day. In fact, He said: "I know the thoughts I think towards you, thoughts of peace and not of evil, to give you an expected end." Yes, you are on the mind of The Creator God, and He's going to do you good. Apostle Paul declared: "It is God that is working in you both to will and to do of His good pleasure." Declare today as the Psalmist did: "Many, O Lord my God, are thy wonderful works which thou has done, and thy thoughts which are to us-ward: they cannot be reckoned up in order unto thee: if I would declare and speak of them, they are than can be numbered." You are the apple of God's eye, and nothing can pluck you out of His hands. Enjoy the favor.

Daily Prayer

Father God, thank you for always having me in mind and thinking of me at all times, in Jesus' Name, Amen.

PROVEN BY THE FIRE

"Behold, I have refined thee, but not with silver; I have chosen thee in the furnace of affliction."

Isaiah 48:10 (KJV)

God can use your battles and attacks of the enemy to strengthen and mature you. Apostle James declared: "Brethren, count it all joy when you fall into divers temptations; knowing this, that the trying of your faith worketh patience. But let patience have her perfect work, that ye may be perfect and entire wanting nothing." Your struggles, battles, wars, attacks, and fights will serve to mature you and grow your faith. Your scars from your wars and battles are nothing but testimonies to what God has delivered you from. No, God did not choose you from a soft place or a high place but rather from the furnace of affliction. You have a testimony, and you can use it to remind the enemy of what God can do through you.

Daily Prayer

Father God, thank you for allowing me to overcome all that would face me in the past and all that will confront me in the future, in Jesus' Name, Amen.

THE ALMIGHTY GOD; NOTHING IS TOO DIFFICULT

"Behold, I am the Lord, the God of all flesh: is there anything too hard for me?"

Jeremiah 32:27 (KJV)

Always remind the enemy that if God does not do a thing, He is certainly able to do it. And, if He does not do something, you will still praise His Holy Name. Let the enemy know that you will bless the Lord at all times and that His praise shall continue to be in your mouth. In fact, declare as the young Hebrew men did: "If it be so, our God whom we serve is able to deliver us from the burning fiery furnace, and He will deliver us out of thine hand, O king." Remember, "God is able to do exceeding abundantly above all that you can ask or think according to the power that worketh in you." There is absolutely nothing too difficult or hard for the Lord to do.

Daily Prayer

Father God, thank you that you are always greater than what confronts me and for always giving me a way of escape, in the Name of Jesus, Amen.

RESTORED BY CHRIST

"For a just man falleth seven times, and riseth up again: but the wicked shall fall into mischief."

Proverbs 24:16 (KJV)

God is not just a God of a second chance. He is longsuffering, not willing that any man should perish but that he or she should come into the knowledge of the truth. Your destiny is not going to change because of setbacks or mistakes. You may struggle because of them, but your God-given destiny will remain the same. Gifts and callings are without repentance, meaning that God will not change His mind about the gifts He has given you or what He has called you to do. If you have fallen, get up. If you missed it, try again. If you failed, start over. Your life is not in the hands any man; God is the "Author and Finisher of your faith," not any man or thing.

Daily Prayer

Father God, thank you for always being a forgiving God and for restoring me after each failure, in the Name of Jesus, Amen.

FAITHFULNESS OF THE LORD

"If we believe not, yet He abideth faithful: He cannot deny Himself."
2 Timothy 2:13 (KJV)

The Lord is faithful even when we are not, for He cannot deny Himself. He is the same yesterday, today, and forever. When we fail Him, He is still faithful to His Word. His promises are never altered, His will is unchangeable, His grace is always free, and His mercy is everlasting. He is faithful and will establish you and keep you from evil. He is faithful, and His faithfulness does not depend upon yours. That's the kind of God He is, and that's the power of His grace and mercy. The Lord is far greater than anything that you do or don't do. Never worry – He has no days off and never sleeps. No matter what you do or say, God is bound by His Word, and He cannot deny Himself. Rejoice.

Daily Prayer

Father God, thank you for always being a faithful God and for never forsaking or leaving me, in the Name of Jesus, Amen.

IN HIS HANDS

"Wherefore, if God so clothe the grass of the field, which today is, and tomorrow is cast into the oven, shall He not much more clothe you, O ye of little faith?"

Matthew 6:30 (KJV)

If God takes care of the birds that have no homes, He can take care of you. If God can make the flowers grow and remain beautiful, He can certainly bless and keep you. Worrying about tomorrow is a waste of your God-given time because tomorrow will take care of itself. It's great looking for something to come later; expectation is fuel for motivation. However, don't forget to embrace what is available and happening today. What God has given you today—opportunities to grow, to share, to start over, to renew, to forgive, to plant that seed. This is the day that the Lord has made; rejoice and be glad in it. Today was made for you; take full advantage of its offerings.

Daily Prayer

Father God, thank you for being the God of my now and future, always providing all my need, in Jesus' Name, Amen.

HE IS ALWAYS PRESENT

"Whither shall I go from thy Spirit? Or whither shall I flee from thy presence."

Psalms 139:7 (KJV)

Where you go, good places or bad ones, God is there. Wherever you go, He will be there. You will not go through anything without His presence. Your way may not be easy, but it is through Him that you continue to go forward. He is always a present help in the time of trouble. Declare as the Psalmist did: "If I ascend up into the heaven, thou art there: if I make my bed in hell, behold, thou art there. If I take the wings of the morning, and dwell in the uttermost parts of the sea; even there shall thy hand lead me, and thy right hand shall hold me." Also, "Fear not, for He is with you; be not dismayed, for He is your God. He will help you; He will strengthen you; He will uphold you with the right hand of His righteousness." Trust and believe Him today.

Daily Prayer

Father God, thank you that I can rest assured that your presence will always go with me, regardless of where I may find myself, in the Name of Jesus, Amen.

NEVER FORGOTTEN

"Remember these, O Jacob and Israel; for thou art my servant: I have formed thee; thou art my servant: O Israel, thou shalt not be forgotten of me."

Isaiah 44:21 (KJV)

God will never run out of blessings. There are some left for you, not just today, but in the future as well. And, He does not need permission, approval, or the aid of man to cause a blessing to come upon you. Others my count you out, but God never will. The Lord is a present help at all times. We know because of His Word that "He is a sun and shield; He will give grace and glory." Don't be dismayed, but encourage yourself in the Lord. In fact, be encouraged now in the Name of Jesus. Your situation or circumstance or position is no match for the grace, favor, or glory of the Lord. You cannot outlast, outrun, or outdo the love, glory, mercy, or will of the Father. You will never be forgotten by Him; today is no exception.

Daily Prayer

Father God, thank you for keeping me in your mind and for causing me to never be forgotten, regardless of my current status, in the Name of Jesus, Amen.

IN HIS WILL

"In whom also we have obtained an inheritance, being predestinated according to the purpose of Him who worketh all things after the counsel of His own will."

Ephesians 1:11 (KJV)

When God chose you, He chose your path, purpose, destiny, and even the family that you were born into. It is up to you to follow the leading of the Holy Spirit to realize the full weight and benefits of who and what He made you to be and to do. Please don't settle until you do. If the day does not seem to be going your way, remind yourself that Jesus is still the way, regardless. Remember, you are always in His hands and always under His grace and mercy. He knows your down sitting and your uprising and understands all of your thoughts. He knows your path and position and is acquainted with all of your way. He's always the same and will always be the same.

Daily Prayer

Father God, thank you for always working things out for me according to your will for me, in the Name of Jesus, Amen.

MY EVERYTHING

"The Lord is my rock, and my fortress, and my deliverer; and God, my strength, in whom I will trust; my buckler, and the horn of my salvation, and my high tower."

Psalms 18:2 (KJV)

Today, declare and acknowledge that God is your rock, and you can stand solidly upon Him. If you are hurting today, know that God can and will make a way for you. It's His promise, and He will not forget any of His promises to you. Let Him know that you are hurting, that you are disappointed, that you feel forsaken, that you feel alone, that you don't understand why certain things are happening; for He is your Father, and He is not threatened by your questions. He loves you and is going to comfort you. He will keep you in perfect peace if you keep your mind centered upon Him. He is all that you need Him to be: rock, fortress, deliverer, strength, buckler, salvation, and God Almighty. Yes, He is everything, even beyond description.

Daily Prayer

Father God, thank you for being my everything; regardless of my situation, you are always my answer, in Jesus' Name, Amen.

BENEFIT OF TRUSTING HIM

"Trust in the Lord, and do good; so shalt thou dwell in the land, and verily thou shalt be fed."

Psalms 37:3 (KJV)

Trust in the Lord at all times and pour out your heart before Him. You can trust Him for all your need, regardless of the severity or size of your request. You can trust Him with your troubles, your need, and all your problems. The Psalmist declared: "And they that know thy name will put their trust in thee: for thou, Lord, hast not forsaken them that seek thee. Some trust in chariots, and some in horses: but we will remember the Name of the Lord." You can trust Him at all times for all things. Cast all of your cares upon Him, for He cares for you and will take care of you. The Lord can block every plan, every scheme, and every device that the enemy will try on today. Trust Him for everything today.

Daily Prayer

Father God, in thee do I put all my trust for all that I need and desire, in the Name of Jesus, Amen.

THE BLESSING OF THE UPRIGHT

"For thou, Lord, wilt bless the righteous; with favour wilt thou compass him as with a shield."

Psalms 5:12 (KJV)

Job declared: "Thou hast granted me with life and favour, and thy visitation hath preserved my spirit." There is a blessing in walking in righteousness. David declared: "For the Lord God is a sun and shield: the Lord will give grace and glory: no good thing will He withhold from them that walk uprightly." The favour that God has for you on today will far exceed anything with which the enemy will confront you. You need not worry. Favour will be with you all day in spite of your situation or condition. You will not face anything alone; God will be there every step of the way, for He has promised to never leave nor forsake you. You can take Him at His Word.

Daily Prayer

Father God, thank you for favoring me on today and for providing all my needs, through Christ Jesus, Amen.

WHEN WE PRAISE

"Let the people praise thee, O God; let all the people praise thee. Then shall the earth yield her increase; and God, even our own God, shall bless us."

Psalms 67:5-6 (KJV)

King David declared: "I will bless the Lord at all times, His praise shall continuously be in my mouth." The Word lets us know that God inhabits the praises of His people. When we praise, the presence of the Lord is manifested in our midst. Praise in an invitation for the Lord to come and set in our presence and make His abode with us. The Psalmist declared: "Let the people praise thee. O God; let all the people praise thee. O let the nations be glad and sing for joy: for thou shalt judge the people righteously, and govern the nations upon the earth. Let the people praise thee, O God; let all the people praise thee. Then the earth shall yield her increase; and God, even our own God, shall bless us. God shall bless us; and all the ends of the earth shall fear Him."

Daily Prayer

Father God, I praise you for your goodness, your grace, your mercy, and all that you continue to do for me, in the Name of Jesus, Amen.

WE ARE CHOSEN

"But ye are a chosen generation, a royal priesthood, an holy nation, a peculiar people; that ye should shew forth the praises of Him who hath called you out of darkness into His marvelous light."

1 Peter 2:9 (KJV)

God created you in His image and after His likeness. You are fearfully and wonderfully made. He chose you to bear His likeness and image. Apostle Paul declared in his letter to the church in Ephesus: "According as He hath chosen us in Him before the foundation of the world, that we should be holy and without blame before Him in love. Having predestinated us into the adoption of children by Jesus Christ to Himself, according to the good pleasure of His will. God did this through our Lord and Savior, Jesus Christ. Yes, you are chosen, royal, holy, and peculiar all because God chose to make you as such even before the foundation of the world.

Daily Prayer

Father God, thank you for caring enough about me to include me in your divine plans in the kingdom, in Jesus' Name, Amen.

NO FAILURE IN GOD

"Be strong and of a good courage, fear not, nor be afraid of them: for the Lord thy God, He it is that doth go with thee; He will not fail thee, nor forsake thee."

Deuteronomy 31:6 (KJV)

Regardless of who or what is against you, know for a certainty that God is for you and on your side. If God is for you, then who can be against you? Greater is He that is within you than he that is in the world. Declare today that no weapon that is formed against me shall not prosper, and I will overcome all that the enemy throws at me. Regardless of what you may face, know that you will not face it alone. In spite of situations or circumstances, grace will empower you, strengthen you, and see you through all that you will face today. Be strong and of good courage, for the Lord is with you and for you.

Daily Prayer

Father God, I praise you in advance for strengthening me to face all that the enemy will try and attack me with on today, in Jesus' Name, Amen.

HIS PRESENCE WILL GO WITH YOU

"Yea, though I walk through the valley of the shadow of death, I will fear no evil: for thou art with me; they rod and thy staff they comfort me."

Psalms 23:4 (KJV)

In God's presence is the fullness of joy and life evermore. It matters not what you are in or what the situation might be, the Word of God said that God will deliver you out of them. Your valley experience or low point was not a waste of time; for it was there that you became grounded and settled. Paise God for where you came from, for it did help shape you and lend directions to your current status. God did and will work out all things together for your good, and the enemy is helpless to do anything about it. Don't worry. Though you may have valley experience on today, God will be there to bring you out. Trust Him today.

Daily Prayer

Father God, thank you for always being my present help at all times, in the Name of Jesus, Amen.

SUPERNATURAL STRENGTH

"For by thee I have run through a troop: by my God have I leaped over a wall."

2 Samuel 22:30 (KJV)

God, and your faith in Him, makes all things possible. God takes your natural abilities and supplies His power and presence and makes supernatural come upon you. Apostle Paul declared: "I can do all things through Christ that strengthens me." We know that "God is able to do exceeding abundantly above all that we can ask or think according to the power that worketh in us." This coupled with our faith, makes nothing impossible unto us. If we can ask it, God can do it; if we can think it, God can bring it to pass; if we can plan it, God is able to bring it to pass. There is nothing too hard for God, and nothing is impossible to them that believe. Believe God's Word.

Daily Prayer

Father God, thank you for empowering me to do what you have purposed me to do, in the Name of Jesus, Amen.

DIVINE SECURITY

"Hear my voice, O God, in my prayer: preserve my life from fear of the enemy."

Psalms 64:1 (KJV)

God is your strength, your shield, your protector, and your hiding place. The enemy would love for you to walk in fear, hoping that you will not pursue your God-given purpose. Fear can come upon you; doubt may arise; the uncertainty about what's happening can make the best of us wonder; loneliness can creep in out of nowhere. Sometimes it appears that our strength is not there; even our faith seems to fade at times. Yet, we must believe and know that God is there with us every step of the way, no matter how we feel. Today, declare as the Prophet Isaiah did: "Fear thou not; for I am with thee: be not dismayed; for I am thy God: I will help thee; yea, I will uphold thee with the right hand of my righteousness." The Lord will keep and preserve you today.

Daily Prayer

Father God, thank you for being my strength in battle, my shield in war, and my way to victory, in the Name of Jesus', in Amen.

FAVORED AND BLESSED, TODAY

"For thou art the glory of their strength: and in thy favour our horn shall be exalted."

Psalms 89:17 (KJV)

Declare today that God's favor is on me....favor for success, favor to overcome, favor for promotion, favor to conquer, favor to begin again. Declare that the "time to favor me has come." You are blessed and highly favored—favored to overcome, favored to prosper, favored to achieve all that God has purposed you to do. Declare as Job did: "Thou has granted me life and favour, and thy visitation hath preserved my spirit." You can do all things through Christ who strengthens you. It's one of the benefits of His favor. Enjoy it, embrace it, and live in it. Know today that a good man obtaineth favour of the Lord, and no good thing will He withhold from them who walketh uprightly.

Daily Prayer

Father God, thank you for your divine favor that is with me in all that I have to encounter, in Jesus' Name.

GOD'S BEST FOR YOU

"Remember me, O Lord, with the favour that thou bearest unto thy people: O visit me with thy salvation."

Psalms 106:4 (KJV)

God will never forget the promises that He has made to you. He will never overlook or skip over you when it is your time to be blessed. Expect God's best, look for His favor, receive His grace, and settle for nothing less. You have got to believe that what's coming is better than what has been. A simple yet powerful truth is "The Lord will make a way!" You may not know or be able to say how, when, or where, but you know that He will make a way, even when there does not even seem to be a way. Don't allow time to shake your faith and doubt God; what's coming will come, and it will not delay. They that wait for the Lord shall renew their strength. Declare this to be what you will testify to on today.

Daily Prayer

Father God, thank you for being what I need, all I need, and when I need it, every day, in the Name of Jesus, Amen.

MEETING EXPECTATIONS

"I had fainted, unless I had believed to see the goodness of the Lord in the land of the living."

Psalms 27:13 (KJV)

God is your hope – hope that you can build on, plan on, and operate on now. You can believe and expect as Abraham did, who against hope believed in hope. You must believe that you are too close to something great and awesome to stop, quit, give up, or even slow down now. The intensity of your battle is a tip that you are about to overcome. You can say this morning as the Psalmist did: "If it had not been the Lord who was on our side, when men rose up against us: then they had swallowed us up quick, when their wrath was kindled against us: Then the water had overwhelmed us, the stream had gone over our soul: Then the proud waters had gone over our soul. Blessed be the Lord, who hath not given us as prey to their teeth."

Daily Prayer

Father God, thank you for always going beyond my expectations, and never leaving me at the mercy of my enemies, in the Name of Jesus, Amen.

IT WILL COME TO PASS

"God is not a man, that He should lie; neither the son of man, that He should repent: hath He said, and shall He not do it? Or hath He spoken, and shall He not make it good?"

Numbers 23:19 (KJV)

God will not nor can He ever lie. He will not miss an appointment, forget a promise, make a mistake, or need to be reminded of His Word. He will fulfill every promise, direct every step, hear every cry, supply every need, fight every battle with you, provide daily bread, and send grace to every situation and circumstance. Why? Because these are His promises, and He cannot lie. Keep in mind that if God said it, you know that it shall come to pass. You can rest assured today that God will fulfill every promise made to you, for He swore by His own Name that what He has promised or said will be done or come to pass. This is His promise for you, too.

Daily Prayer

Father God, thank you for always being faithful to your Word and to all of your promises, in the Name of Jesus, Amen.

LIVING TRIUMPHANTLY

"For thou, Lord, hast made me glad through thy work: I will triumph in the works of thy hands."

Psalms 92:4 (KJV)

Do your best to work and serve with what you currently have until you get what is necessary or needed for your total success. Excuses or "I don't have" are not options. The way may not be easy, but if God is doing the leading, you will ascend to the heights that you were born to reach. Apostle Paul declared to the church at Corinth: "Now thanks be unto God, which always causeth us to triumph in Christ, and maketh manifest the savour of his knowledge by us in every place." Moreover, "It is Christ that works in you both to will and to do of His good pleasure." Therefore, you have all you need to succeed in every area of your life, not just today, but for life.

Daily Prayer

Father God, thank you for always making me triumph over my enemies, regardless of the battle, in the Name of Jesus, Amen.

HAVING ALL SUFFICIENCY

"And God is able to make all grace abound toward you; that ye, always having all sufficiency in all things, may abound go every good work."
2 Corinthians 9:8 (KJV)

God gave us His best, Jesus Christ, to redeem us. There's no way He will ever give you anything less now. The scripture reminds us that "Though He was rich, yet He became poor that we through His poverty might be rich." Expect them, embrace them, and enjoy the many benefits that God has made available to you. Since God has made all of this available, live life to the fullest. Don't look back. What was left behind will always be there. Know that whatever is of God will overcome. What is God-given will be God-protected. This is the day for increase, the day for promotion, the day for blessings, the day for supernatural favor and grace. Enjoy the benefits of God today; they were made especially for you.

Daily Prayer

Father God, thank you for gracing me to overcome all that will confront me on today, in the name of Jesus, Amen.

HE IS MY LIFE

"O Lord, by these things men live, and in all these things is the life of my spirit: so wilt thou recover me, and make me to live."

Isaiah 38:16 (KJV)

Today can be your day of recovery! The enemy will not know when God will give you an amazing victory! Don't quit, don't back down, but keep moving forward. You can overcome, for "Greater is He that is within you, than he that is in the world." Stay focused, stay strong, stay committed, keep the faith. The distractions will be over soon. Serving the Lord will pay off for you. Stay faithful, and keep laboring in the vineyard. Recovery is coming. You are made in the image and likeness of God, fearfully made. Look for it, plan on it, and expect it to come. Recovery is in your future, regardless of what your current situation might be.

Daily Prayer

Father God, thank you for giving me new life every day and for leading me in the path that you have planned for me, in Jesus' Name, Amen.

HE SEES ME NOT AS MAN DOES

"...for the Lord seeth not as man seeth; for man looketh on the outward appearance, but the Lord looketh on the heart."

1 Samuel 16:7(b) (KJV) "

You don't have to be known by man to be called and used by God. Popularity with man does not mean the approval of God. Thank goodness He does not see us as man does. If there is a call on you, say "yes" and allow the Holy Spirit to direct you to the proper covering. God does not need the approval, the opinion, or the blessings of others to use you for His glory. Man can look at the outward appearance of someone and choose to use or not use them, but God sees what is in the heart and uses whom He chooses to use in His Kingdom. Remember, "A man's gift will make room for him, and bring him before great men." It's what God has given you and not what man thinks about you that's important.

Daily Prayer

Father God, thank you for considering me for use in your Kingdom and for using me in any manner, in Jesus' Name, Amen.

STAYING IN HIS WILL

"And the world passeth away, and the lust thereof: but he that doeth the will of God abideth for ever."

1 John 2:17 (KJV)

If you want God's best for your life, seek the will of God; for whatever God wants, He wills it. And, who can stop the "WILL" of God. Apostle Paul lets us know that it "is God that worketh in us both to will and to do of His good pleasure." When he wants His will to be done, He simply gives you a want or desire for that particular thing. Learn and do the will of God; it will get you what God wants for your life. Knowing and doing the will of God will cause success in all that you have been given to do. Knowing the will of God will also cause your faithfulness to be manifested for all to see, thereby giving glory to the Lord. Doing the Will of God will give you staying power like nothing else can.

Daily Prayer

Father God, please help me to remain faithful to doing your will, not just today, but at all times, in Jesus' Name, Amen.

WE ARE HIS PEOPLE

"For the Lord will not forsake His people for His great Name's sake: because it hast pleased the Lord to make you His people."

1 Samuel 12:22 (KJV)

For His Name's sake, the Lord will never forget, forsake, or fail His people. What God has for you is unstoppable. Your enemy, position, or situation will not interfere with what's coming. He will supply all of your need according to His riches in glory through Christ Jesus. Expect this to happen. Be encouraged, God has not forgotten about you. Be encouraged, the promise is still good. In the fullness of time, your blessing, your breakthrough, your promotion, your miracle will come or take place. Don't worry or fret – the God who holds time in His hands never misses and appointment or breaks a promise. The enemy is helpless to stop what is promised to you.

Daily Prayer

Father God, thank you for considering me and for keeping me in mind, regardless of my position or situation, in the Name of Jesus, Amen.

LIFTED UP AGAIN

"Thou hast turned for me my mourning into dancing: thou hast put off my sackcloth, and girded me with gladness."

Psalms 30:11 (KJV)

The Lord wants to and will revive us again. He wants to turn our mourning into a celebration. Don't allow the disappointment to dampen your spirit, crush your hope, stir up doubt, or cause you to entertain the thoughts of giving up; you could still be just one person, one yes, one idea away from total victory! The Psalmist declared: "Lift up your heads, O ye gates; and be ye lifted up, ye everlasting doors; and he King of Glory shall come in." Declare today as Isaiah did: "Therefore, the redeemed of the Lord shall return, and come with singing unto Zion; and everlasting joy shall be upon their head: they shall obtain gladness and joy; and sorrow and mourning shall flee away." It's your time; decree it as so today.

Daily Prayer

Father God, thank you for turning my darkness into light, my sadness into joy, and my lack into abundance, in the Name of Jesus, Amen.

UNWAVERING FAITH

"He staggered not at the promise of God through unbelief; but was strong in faith, giving glory to God."

Romans 4:20 (KJV)

We all need to take the example left to us by Abraham who against hope believed in hope, that he might become the father of many nations; according to that which was spoken, so shall thy seed be. And being not weak in faith, he considered not his own body now dead, when he was about an hundred years old, neither yet the deadness of Sara's womb: He staggered not at the promise of God through unbelief; but was strong in faith, giving glory to God; And being fully persuaded that, what He had promised, He was able also to perform. The promises that God made to you are still good and always will be, no matter what it looks like now. Just believe.

Daily Prayer

Father God, please help me to continue to walk by faith and not by what my natural eyes see, in the Name of Jesus, Amen.

GROWING IN GRACE

"But grow in grace and in the knowledge of our Lord and Saviour Jesus Christ. To Him be glory both now and for ever. Amen."

2 Peter 3:18 (KJV)

What you feed will grow; therefore, it is good to feed your faith and starve your doubt. Apostle Paul declared: "And be not conformed to this world: but be ye transformed by the renewing of your mind, that ye may prove what is that good, and acceptable, and perfect, will of God." By doing this, we will feed our spirit man and starve the flesh so that we can better know the will of the Father. What you feed will grow, and what you starve will eventually die. It is through Christ, that we live, move, and have our being. God has graced us today, and this grace will empower us to achieve what we have been given to do, in the Name of Jesus.

Daily Prayer

Father God, thank you for your grace and for never allowing my enemy to have an upper hand on me, in Jesus' Name, Amen.

FORGIVE US

"Remember not the sins of my youth, nor my transgressions: according to thy mercy remember thou me for thy goodness' sake, O Lord."

Psalms 25:7 (KJV)

Through the sacrifice of Jesus Christ, we have been forgiven and justified with God. Apostle Paul stated in Ephesians: "In whom we have redemption through His blood, the forgiveness of sins, according to the riches of His grace." Paul further stated: "And you, being dead in your sins and the uncircumcision of your flesh, hath he quickened together with him, having forgiven you all trespasses; blotting out he handwriting of ordinances that was against us, which was contrary to us, and took it out of the way, nailing it to His cross." Through the grace of God, through Christ, you have been made free. Enjoy this freedom today and forever.

Daily Prayer

Father God, thank you for forgiving me of all my past sin and giving me right standing with the Father, in Jesus' Name, Amen.

TRUSTING GOD THROUGH FEAR

"What time I am afraid, I will trust in thee."

Psalms 56:3 (KJV)

We know that "God has not given us the spirit of fear, but of power, and of love, and of a sound mind." However, fear will become a reality for most of us at one time or another. Fear also has torment, tormenting those who are given prey to it. We must keep in mind also that fear is a spirit, and it can be rebuked and rejected. And, since God did not give it, you do not have to allow it to be a part of your daily struggle. The enemy is behind all fears, and his intention is to make you draw back, give up, and turn back. When you are feeling the attacks of fear, trust God for answers, directions, comfort, and protection. Declare as David did: "Yea as I walk through the valley of the shadow of death, I will fear no evil because thou (the Lord) art with me." He is your protector.

Daily Prayer

Father God, thank you for your direction, comfort, and protection, as we reject fear in our lives, in Jesus' Name, Amen.

DOUBLE FAVOR

"For your shame ye shall have double: and for confusion they shall rejoice in their portion: therefore, in their land they shall possess the double: everlasting joy shall be unto them."

Isaiah 61:7 (KJV)

Don't get tired of doing what you know is right, for in your due season, you will reap what you have sown. As a believer, you can expect to receive a harvest from sowing into the lives of others. It's the law of the Kingdom. Moreover, you are enccouraged to "give, and it shall be given unto you; good measures, pressed down, shaken together, and running over, shall men give unto your bosom." Both of these are principles of the law of the Kingdom, and nothing can change it. Because of what the enemy has stolen and what you have had to endure, you are in line for double return. And, for confusion, rejoicing will be given unto you. Expect and receive it as done.

Daily Prayer

Father God, thank you for the harvest that is coming to me, even the ones that the enemy has held back or stolen, in the Name of Jesus, Amen.

CREATED FOR SUCCESS

"For we are His workmanship, created in Christ Jesus unto good works, which God hath before ordained that we should walk in them."

Ephesians 2:10 (KJV)

We were created in the image and likeness of God, and we can be certain that we were not created for failure. God has not, cannot, nor will He ever make a mistake. You have been created for greatness and success. Regardless of your current situation, condition, or position, you are blessed and highly favored. God has no plan "B" for your life; He does not need one. He is the Potter and you are His clay. If necessary, He will make you into another vessel to achieve His original purpose for your life! Your current situation does not frighten Him; your current position does not change His plans for you; your current circumstance does not cancel out the purpose that God has for you. Yes, you are His workmanship, created for good works.

Daily Prayer

Father God, thank you for working in me to complete the work that I have been given to do, in the Name of Jesus, Amen.

NEVER WILL BE FORSAKEN

"I have been young, and now am old; yet have I not seen the righteous for-saken, nor his seed begging bread."

Psalms 37:25 (KJV)

No matter where you go, what you do, or in what position you may find yourself, you will never be forsaken. The Psalmist made this extremely clear when he wrote that he has never seen the righteous forsaken, and not even his seed would have to beg for bread. He further declared: "No good thing will God withhold from them that walk uprightly." When things are not going well or seemingly in your favor, know that God is still in your corner. When disappointment comes out of nowhere, know that He is a present help in the time of trouble. You are not and never will be alone. Believe today that God is going to make all things, good and not so good, work together for your good in the end. Stay faithful, for the faithful shall abound in blessings.

Daily Prayer

Father God, thank you for always being right by my side meeting all my need, in Jesus' Name, Amen.

MY CONFIDANTE

"Though an host should encamp against me, my heart shall not fear: though war should rise against me, in this will I be confident."

Psalms 27:3 (KJV)

Always remember, regardless of the situation or circumstance, the "Greater Than" is for you. He is always more than enough, regardless of whom the battle is with. Being called and chosen by God does not mean that you will not have enemies, face some difficulties, or maybe even suffer some losses; but it does mean that God will provide what you need to succeed and overcome every obstacle that you will face. The Psalmist made this clear when he stated: "Many are the afflictions of the righteous, yet God does deliver him out of them all." Rest assured in knowing that God did not call you to fail. You can do all things through Christ who strengthens you. Succeed in the Name of Jesus.

Daily Prayer

Father God, thank you for always being more than enough for me and always being bigger than my enemies, in the Name of Jesus, Amen.

IN HIS AUTHORITY

"The Lord sitteth upon the flood; yea, the Lord sitteth King for ever. The Lord will give strength unto His people; the Lord will bless His people with peace."
Psalms 29:10-11 (KJV)

Thank God that His peace, which surpasses all understanding, is greater than the situations or circumstances in which we may find ourselves. His peace is not based upon what we have but in spite of what we have or don't have. He will keep us in perfect peace if we keep our minds stayed on Him. Thank God for favor – it is priceless. God daily loads us with awesome gifts, and nothing or no one can stop them from getting to us. We can rejoice in knowing that God is the same yesterday, today, and forever. Yes, the Lord will give you strength on today, and His peace that He has for you will surpass all your understanding. Enjoy these benefits today.

Daily Prayer

Father God, thank you for your wonderful blessings that you give to me on a daily basis, in the Name of Jesus, Amen.

THE EVERLASTING WORD

"The grass withereth, the flower fadeth: but the word of our God shall stand for ever."

Isaiah 40:8 (KJV)

The Word of God has been tried and tested and is still true, ever-lasting, and unchanged. According the Apostle Paul, the Holy Scriptures are able to "make thee wise unto salvation through faith which is in Christ Jesus. All scripture is given by inspiration of God, and is profitable for doctrine, for reproof, for correction, for instruction in righteousness. That the man of God may be perfect, thoroughly furnished unto all good works." This is the power of the unchanging Word of God. The Hebrews writer states that all things are held together by the power of God's word. The words of others cannot overrule the Word of God. God can and will always keep His Word. Trust Him today to do all that He promised in His Word.

Daily Prayer

Father God, thank you for your Word and the life that it brings to me every day, in the Name of Jesus, Amen.

THE GLORY OF THE LORD

"Arise, shine; for thy light is come, and the glory of the Lord is risen upon thee."

Isaiah 60:1 (KJV)

We were made in the image and likeness of God, created to bring Him glory. We are the apple of God's eye and are loved by Him unconditionally. Nothing can separate us from this unconditional love. On the days that are not good, we must remember that God is good and always will be. When darkness tries to engulf us, we should declare that He is the light that shines within us. When we are feeling discouraged, we should declare as Isaiah did: "To appoint unto them that mourn in Zion, to give unto them beauty for ashes, the oil of joy for mourning, the garment of praise for the spirit of heaviness." Yes, He is the Light that shines in our lives every day.

Daily Prayer

Father God, thank you for allowing the light of your countenance to shine forth on me every day, in the Name of Jesus, Amen.

IN HIS THOUGHTS

"How precious also are thy thoughts unto me, O God! How great is the sum of them!"

Psalms 139:17 (KJV)

You are always on the mind of God. The Prophet Jeremiah declared: "I know the thoughts that I think toward you, saith the Lord, thoughts of peace, and not of evil, to give you an expected end." You do not have to compete for God's attention. You are always on the mind of God. And, since you are on His mind, you are always just a word or prayer away from His provisions and assistance. Apostle Paul stated: "He that spared not His own Son, but delivered Him up for all, how shall He not with Him freely give us all things?" You can go "boldly to the throne of grace, that you may obtain mercy, and find grace to help in the time of need." God is always thinking of you.

Daily Prayer

Father God, thank you for keeping me in your thoughts and for having plans to prosper me every day, in Jesus' Name, Amen.

SUFFERING FOR HIS GLORY

"Yet if any man suffer as a Christian, let him not be ashamed; but let him glorify God on this behalf."

1 Peter 4:16 (KJV)

Trouble does not mean that God is not with you or for you; it simply means that your enemy does not want you to fulfill what God as given you to do. On the other hand, the absence of trouble does not mean it's God-sent. Pray for the spirit of discernment in all these things. The presence of struggles or attacks from the enemy does not mean the absence of God's presence or His disapproval. Apostle Paul declared: "Yea, all that will live godly in Christ Jesus shall suffer persecution." The Apostle Peter declared: "Wherefore let them that suffer according to the will of God commit the keeping of their soul to Him in well doing, as unto a faithful Creator. Yes, through all that you may encounter, know that God will get the glory out of it.

Daily Prayer

Father God, help me to endure what you allow to confront me that you get the glory out of my life, in the Name of Jesus, Amen.

ALWAYS PRESENT

"We thank you, O God! We give thanks because you are near. People every-where tell of your wonderful deeds."

Psalms 75: 1 (NLT)

O give thanks unto the Lord, for He is good, He is good. Praise God that we do not have to face today's issues alone! We may not know what today holds, but we can be certain that grace and mercy will be there to assist us every step of the way. Come what may, The Lord will not take His eyes off of us at any time throughout the day. What a blessing. Declare today that "God will perfect all that concerns me." Decree today that no opportunity will bypass me; no open door will be off limits to me; and God's favor will overshadow and overpower all that come against me! Know also that God did not bring you out to forsake you now. He did not raise you up to make you fail. He has not called you without a plan to prosper and protect you. Enjoy!

Daily Prayer

Father God, thank you for being my shelter and strength for all that I need and encounter, in the Name of Jesus, Amen.

NOTHING IS IMPOSSIBLE

"O Sovereign Lord! You made the heavens and earth by your strong hand and powerful arm. Nothing is too hard for you!"

Jeremiah 32:17 (NLT)

Jesus said that nothing is impossible to them that believe – nothing. Without Christ, we can do nothing. With Christ, we can do all things that He strengthens us to do. We can rest assured that what God begins will succeed. Nothing, not one thing, is too hard for Him to do. Whatever is needed to succeed, He will provide. He never gives visions without attaching provisions with them. Blessings are in our future, and only time stands between them and us. Moreover, since God can change the times and the seasons, the blessings could come at any moment. It's His will to bless us. Nothing is impossible to them that believe, and nothing is too big for God to make come to pass. Make known His deeds among His people. Glory to God

Daily Prayer

Father God, thank you for your awesome power, and for always being a present help to me regardless of my situation, in the Name of Jesus, Amen.

FOLLOWING THE TEACHING

"Those things, which ye have both learned, and received, and heard, and seen in me, do: and the God of peace shall be with you."

Philippians 4:9 (KJV)

In difficult and tough times, remember they will not last; in great times, stay humble; in trying times, stay positive; in low moments, lift up your eyes to where your help comes from. Remember the things that God has brought you through; let them be a testimony to fight any future attacks of the enemy. The Apostle John declared: "And they overcame him by the blood of the Lamb, and by the word of their testimony; and they loved not their lives unto the death." Your testimonies can give you peace against the attacks of the enemy, knowing that if God brought you through before, He will do it again. Come what may, know that God is a present help in times of trouble.

Daily Prayer

Father God, thank you for giving me testimonies that I can use to remind the enemy of your delivering power today, in the Name of Jesus, Amen.

FRUITS OF THE KINGDOM

"For the Kingdom of God is not meat and drink; but righteousness, and peace, and joy in the Holy Ghost."

Romans 14:17 (KJV)

Know for a certainty that the Kingdom of God operates by the Will of God, and man's approval or disapproval is not necessary for it to operate in your life. Man's system does not affect the Kingdom of God. Man's ways are not God's ways nor are man's thoughts His thoughts; as the heavens are higher than the earth, so are God's thoughts higher than man's. He does not need man's methods of doing things to bring increase to your life. The king's heart is in God's hand, and as the river of water, He can turn it whatever way He wills. No, His Kingdom is not meat and drink, but righteousness, peace and joy in the Holy Ghost. He knows how to keep you, provide for you, and lead you in all things concerning His Kingdom. Let Him bless you today.

Daily Prayer

Father God, please help me to live today according to your Kingdom principles, in the Name of Jesus, Amen.

POSITIONED BY THE LORD

"Thou has enlarged by steps under me, that my feet did not slip."
Psalms 18:36 (KJV)

It is through Christ that we live, move, and have our existence. Every good and perfect gift comes from Him, and without Him nothing will take place in our lives. He is the beginning and the end of all things that take place in our lives. Since He is ordering our steps, our obstacles detours, potholes, and roadblocks have to surrender to His plans and will. Being Christ-led will always lead to success according to His purpose, not man's. It is God who establishes us, fixes us, and places us in our proper situations, all to bring Him Glory. Declare as the Psalmist did: "And let the beauty of the Lord our God be upon us: and establish thou the work of our hands upon us; yea, the work of our hands establish thou it." It's the Lord's doing, and it's marvelous in our sight.

Daily Prayer

Father God, thank you for going before me and establishing my path for my day, in the Name of Jesus, Amen.

VICTORY THROUGH CHRIST

"But thanks be to God, which giveth us he victory through our Lord Jesus Christ."

1 Corinthians 15:57 (KJV)

Apostle Paul declared: "Thanks be unto God who always causes us to triumph," and this is possible through Christ Jesus. Rest in knowing that God has declared your end from the beginning, which assures us that our destiny is never in question. The book of Isaiah reminds us that "no weapon that is formed against us will prosper." You can rest in knowing that the Greater Than is on your side, and He is able to do exceeding abundantly above all that you can ask or think according to the power that works in you. The Lord is greater than anything that you will encounter; therefore, victory is yours through Christ Jesus.

Daily Prayer

Father God, thank you for always leading me to victory in all that concerns me, in the Name of Jesus, Amen.

SECURED IN CHRIST

"For the King trusteth in the Lord, and through the mercy of the Most High he shall not be moved."

Psalms 21:7 (KJV)

They that trust in the Lord shall be as mount Zion, which cannot be removed, but abideth forever. You are covered today, covered from the storms, attacks, and any situations that will arise to confront you on to-day. The Psalmist declared: "How the king rejoices in your strength, O Lord. He shouts with joy because you give him victory. For you have given him his heart's desire; you have withheld nothing he requested. You welcomed him back with success and prosperity. You placed a crown of finest gold on his head." He is able to keep you from falling and to present you faultless before the presence of His glory. Rest in His strength today.

Daily Prayer

Father God, thank you for being my strength and my way today, in the Name of Jesus, Amen.

NEW THINGS IN CHRIST

"Behold, I will do a new thing; now it shall spring forth; shall ye not know it? I will even make a way in the wilderness, and rivers in the desert."

Isaiah 43:19 (KJV)

God does not change, but He does do new things in the lives of believers. Yes, He is the same yesterday, today, and forever; but He will do something that has not been done in your life. Trust Him for what is about to take place in your life. Don't allow your "now" position or situation dampen your expectation for increase, promotion, or overall increase. Remember, "The blessing of the Lord, it maketh rich, and He addeth no sorry with it." The day just goes better with Christ. He makes all things new. Know that you have the eye of the Lord looking over you! His eye is on the sparrow, and since it is, you know that He's watching over you.

Daily Prayer

Father God, thank you for doing new things in my life and for showing me the new horizons available to me, in Jesus' Name, Amen.

WHEN IT'S DUE SEASON

"The eyes of all wait upon thee; and thou givest them their meat in due season."

Psalms 145:15 (KJV)

When it is your season for blessings, nothing or no one can stop it. In fact, God will change the times and the seasons just to cause blessings to come upon you. Don't allow the waiting period to cause you to worry or be anxious. God will not be late, overlook you, or forget the promises made to you. He will never miss an assignment or an appointment. You just remain steadfast, unmovable, always abiding in the work of the Lord. Whatever is against you pales in comparison to who is for you. "Wait on the Lord: be of good courage, and He shall strengthen thine heart: wait, I say, on the Lord."

Daily Prayer

Father God, thank you for always being on time for my every need, in the Name of Jesus, Amen.

HE IS THE ANSWER

"He shall call upon me, and I will answer him: I will be with him in trouble; I will deliver him, and honor him."

Psalms 91:15 (KJV)

The Lord said through the Prophet Jeremiah that we could "call unto Him, and He would answer us, and show us great and mighty things, which we knew not of." When fear and doubt are all around us, we can rest assured that grace and mercy will be right there, assisting us with all our needs. Remember the Word of the Lord: "Fear thou not, the Lord is with you; be not dismayed, the Lord is your God; He will strengthen you; He will help you; He will uphold you with the right hand of His righteousness." There will be difficulties, battles, and yes, even a setback or two; but through Christ Jesus, we win. Enjoy His many benefits today.

Daily Prayer

Father God, thank you for delivering me from all my fears and for always keeping me safe through all my storms, in the Name of Jesus, Amen.

DETERMINED BEFORE BIRTH

"Seeing his days are determined, the number of his months are with thee, thou hast appointed his bounds that he cannot pass."

Job 14:5 (KJV)

God has determined your end from the beginning. Know that He is not making things up as you go along. He has plans to prosper you, direct you, and protect you. As a believer, you must know that the "steps of a good man are ordered by the Lord." Declare today that it's working together for my good, regardless of what "it" is. Nothing can undo God's plans for you today. Follow the leading of the Holy Spirit, and you will arrive at your place of purpose on time, in time, and every time. The way out is always through Christ. Know that God's plans and purpose for you are not and will never be in question. The plans for today will be fulfilled

Daily Prayer

Father God, thank you for the plans that you have for my day, plans to prosper and bless me, in the Name of Jesus, Amen.

WE ARE HIS PEOPLE

"Which in time past were not a people, but are now the people of God: which had not obtained mercy, but now have obtained mercy."

1 Peter 2:10 (KJV)

We are the people of God, the apple of His eye, His workmanship, created for good works through Christ. His love is unconditional, and His mercy endureth unto all generations. We are made in His image and likeness to glorify Him in all that we do. The Psalmist declared: "I will praise thee; for I am fearfully and wonderfully made: marvellous are thy works; and that my soul knoweth right well. My substance was not hid from thee, when I was made in secret, and curiously wrought I the lowest parts of the earth." Yes, "We are a chosen generation, a royal priesthood, an holy nation, a particular people; that we should show forth the praises of Him who hath called us out of darkness into His marvellous light." Yes, we are His people, chosen to be so.

Daily Prayer

Father God, thank you for choosing me for your purpose and plans for today, in Jesus' Name, Amen.

COMPLETE IN CHRIST

"The Lord will perfect that which concerneth me: thy mercy, O Lord, endureth for ever: forsake not the works of thine own hands."

Psalms 138:8 (KJV)

Know that God has a plan for your life, and He will complete all that concerns you to fulfill this plan. This plan cannot be stopped or derailed by the will or wishes of man. Your day, and yes, even your life is a process. Please don't quit during the process. It is the process that determines the final outcome of a thing; remember God has determined your end from the beginning. If you will allow God to complete processing you, you will be all that He would have you to be. Don't even entertain the thought of quitting. Don't become weary of doing what is right, for in due time you will reap if you do not quit. Let the enemy know that God will complete all that concerns you without a doubt.

Daily Prayer

Father God, thank you for the work that you are doing in me to fulfill all that you have purposed me to do, in the Name of Jesus, Amen.

BEST IS YET TO COME

"The glory of this latter house shall be greater than of the former, saith the Lord of hosts: and in this place will I give peace, saith the Lord of hosts."

Haggai 2:9 (KJV)

Declare right now that what's coming to me is greater than what has been. No matter how good you think it may have been, greater is coming! No matter your past, greater is coming. How can you know that greater is coming? Because He will never do less for His people. Whatever you need to do, position yourself for greater, for the overflow. He is coming in your direction. The Psalmist declared: "For the Lord God is a sun and shield: the Lord will give grace and glory: no good thing will He withhold from them that walk uprightly." Decree today that what's coming to me is much greater than what has already been in my life. It's coming.

Daily Prayer

Father God, thank you that my best is yet to come – increase, blessings, and favor, in the Name of Jesus', Amen.

FULLY COVERED TODAY

"The Grace of the Lord Jesus Christ, and the love of God, and the communion of the Holy Ghost, be with you all. Amen."

2 Corinthians 13:14 (KJV)

There is no need to fear, worry, doubt, or wonder. God will cover you every second of the day. He will never forsake or leave you, regardless of your situation or position. Nothing can or will separate you from the unconditional love of God by Christ Jesus. And, as long as we have Christ, we have grace; for Christ is the Grace of God. And, His Grace is sufficient for every weakness that you may have. This grace does not need an invitation to show up and do what God has ordained; it just shows up. Because of this amazing grace, declare right now that God will perform all that concerns me today. Declare right now that no enemy I have is greater than the God who is on my side. This grace will be there on time, every time, for you today.

Daily Prayer

Father God, thank you for covering me, protecting me, and providing for me throughout the day, in the Name of Jesus, Amen.

IN GOOD STANDING

"Now unto Him that is able to keep you from falling, and to present you faultless before the presence of His glory with exceeding joy."

Jude 24 (KJV)

God is able to take your worst day and turn it around for your good. There is absolutely nothing too difficult for God to do on your behalf. In fact, He is able to do exceeding abundantly above all that you can ask or think according to the power that worketh in you. God is greater than any of your issues, more powerful than the forces of evil that may confront you. His love is unconditional, and His grace and mercy endureth forever. Moreover, nothing is greater than the power of His Word: "Weeping may endure for a night, but joy cometh in the morning." According to the Hebrew writer, He upholds all things by the power of His Word," and this includes all that confronts you on a regular basis. God is able to do what He said; trust Him.

Daily Prayer

Father God, thank you for enabling me to navigate through all of the traps, distractions, and schemes of the enemy, in the Name of Jesus, Amen.

CLOTHED WITH HIS ARMOUR

"Put on the whole armour of God, that ye may be able to stand against the whiles of the devil."

Ephesians 6:11 (KJV)

God has not left you unprepared to fight the attacks of the enemy. You do not fight against flesh and blood, but against principalities, powers, against rulers of the darkness of this world, and against spiritual wickedness in high places. No matter how you try, you cannot win a spiritual battle with fleshly means. And, The Lord has given you the weapons necessary for you to win: "Stand your ground, putting on the belt of truth and the body of armor of God's righteousness. For shoes, put on the peace that comes from the Good News so that you will be fully prepared. In addition to all of these, hold up the shield of faith to stop the fiery arrows of the devil. Put on salvation as your helmet, and take the sword of the Spirit, which is the Word of God." You are clothed for the battle.

Daily Prayer

Father God, help me to use the weapons you have prepared for me to fight against my enemies, in the Name of Jesus, Amen.

MAKE ALL THINGS AVAILABLE

"I can do all things through Christ which strengtheneth me."
Philippians 4:13 (KJV)

The Prophet Zechariah declared: "This is the word of the Lord unto Zerubbabel, saying, not by might, nor by power, but by my spirit, saith the Lord of hosts." We can do all things through Christ which strengthens us. We can do all things through Him, but nothing without Him. We simply have to supply the faith and allow God to bring to pass what we are seeking. Nothing is impossible to them that believe. It is through Him that we live, move, and have our being. He reminded Apostle Paul that His grace is sufficient, and His strength is made perfect in weakness. God's grace will empower you today to fulfill all that He has purposed you to complete today. Trust Him.

Daily Prayer

Father God, thank you for enabling me to accomplish all that is required of me today, in the Name of Jesus, Amen.

HE DOES NEW THINGS

"Behold, the former things are come to pass, and new things do I declare: before they spring forth I tell you of them."

Isaiah 42:9 (KJV)

He is a God that changes not, yet He can do new things for His people. Declare right now "that my future is too bright to allow what has happened, what should have been, what could have been, or who left me to interfere with what's coming to me!" The best is in front, not behind. There is no victory in looking back, no conquering in thinking what may have been, no overcoming wishing this or that had happened. Don't stop because it gets difficult. The same God who gave you the ability to start will give you the ability to continue. You are blessed and highly favored. God makes all things new; nothing in your past can prevent this from happening.

Daily Prayer

Father God, thank you for always doing new things on my behalf, always making a way for me, in the Name of Jesus, Amen.

EMPOWERED BY CHRIST

"In your strength I can crush an army; with my God I can scale any wall."
Psalms 18:29 (NLT)

All that we are is because of God through Christ. All that we ever will do is because of God through Christ. We can do all things through Christ who strengthens us. In fact, where can we go but to the Lord? The Psalmist declared: "The Lord says, I will guide you along the best path for your life. I will advise you and watch over you." Moreover, the Lord said, "Be still and know that I am God." The writer of the Book of Acts declared: "For in Him we live, and move, and have our being," meaning we are absolutely nothing without Him. The Lord is our source, redeemer, our strong tower, our rewarder, and we can do all things through Christ who strengthens us. Trust Him, regardless of what is going on around you. God will be with you

Daily Prayer

Father God, thank you for being my strength, a strength that enables me to overcome the schemes and attacks of the enemy, in the Name of Jesus, Amen.

HE LIFTS THE DOWNTRODDEN

"From the end of the earth will I cry unto thee, when my heart is overwhelmed: lead me to the rock that is higher than I."

Psalms 61:2 (KJV)

Our hope must be in the Lord; He is our joy, our peace, our comforter, and our protector. The Joy of the Lord is our strength. The Psalmist declared: "Lift up your heads, O ye gates; and be ye lifted up ye everlasting doors; and the King of Glory shall come in. Who is the King of Glory? The Lord strong and mighty, the Lord mighty in battle." He can and will lift up the bowed down head, the troubled spirit, and the soul that is despondent. According Isaiah, the Lord declared: "To appoint unto them that mourn in Zion, to give unto them beauty for ashes, the oil of joy for mourning, the garment of praise for the spirit of heaviness; that they might be called trees of righteousness, the planting of the Lord, that he might be glorified." Be lifted in Jesus' Name.

Daily Prayer

Father God, thank you for always being the lifter up of my head, not allowing me to become overwhelmed by my issues, in the Name of Jesus, Amen.

THE WAIT SHALL BE REWARDED

"Wait on the Lord: be of good courage, and He shall strengthen thine heart: wait, I say, on the Lord."

Psalms 27:14 (KJV)

They that wait upon the Lord shall renew their strength; they shall mount up with wings as eagles; they shall run, and not be weary; and they shall walk, and not faint." The Psalmist declared: "I had fainted, unless I had believed to see the goodness of the Lord in the land of the living. Wait on the Lord: be of good courage, and He shall strengthen thine heart: wait, I say on the Lord." If we wait for the Lord's directions, we will be strengthened and blessed. Patience has its benefits, for the Lord declared in the Book of Hebrews: "For ye have need of patience, that, after ye have done the will of God, ye might receive the promise." Be strengthened.

Daily Prayer

Father God, help me to be patient, willing to wait upon you for all that I need, in the Name of Jesus, Amen.

WATCH AND PRAY

"Watch and pray, that ye enter not into temptation: the spirit indeed is willing, but the flesh is weak."

Matthew 26:41 (KJV)

The Lord Jesus said that "man ought to always pray, and not faint." We see that this is necessary because our spirits are willing but our flesh is weak. Prayer is always in order, never outdated, never old-school. It's always in order. In fact, we are told to always pray. Apostle Paul declared: "Be careful for nothing; but in everything by prayer and supplication with thanksgiving let your requests be made known unto God." The Psalmist declared: "Blessed be God, which hath not turned away my prayer, nor His mercy from me." Remember, "The effectual fervent prayer of the righteous availeth much." Let prayer revive and rejuvenate you today.

Daily Prayer

Father God, guide me through my prayer time that I pray according to your will, in Jesus' Name, Amen.

DELIVERANCE

"And the Lord shall help them, and deliver them: He shall deliver them from the wicked, and save them, because they trust in Him."

Psalms 37:40 (KJV)

God is able to deliver us from all in which we may find ourselves. He is able to deliver from every enemy, every oppression, every bondage, and every battle. He is never late, never too early, and will never leave nor forsake us. King David declared: "When the wicked, even mine enemies and my foes, came upon me to eat up my flesh, they stumbled and fell. Though an host should encamp against me, my heart shall not fear: though war should rise against me, in this will I be confident." If we put our trust in Him, He is able to do all and more than we can ask or think, according to the power that worketh in us. We can be confident that God will deliver us on time, every time.

Daily Prayer

Father God, thank you for always delivering me and leading me in the path of all that I am faced with, in the Name of Jesus, Amen.

ACCORDING TO HIS PLANS

"For it is God which worketh in you both to will and to do of His good pleasure."

Philippians 2:13 (KJV)

God is responsible for causing us to have the desire to please Him and the ability to do what is necessary to fulfill this desire. With that in mind, the struggle may have been a part of the plan. The attack may have been included in the plan all along. Keep in mind that God will complete all that concerns you. Don't get discouraged by what is not happening at the moment; God makes all things work together for good to them that love Him and are the called according to His purpose. Apostle Paul declared: "In whom also we have obtained an inheritance, being predestinated according to the purpose of Him who worketh all things after the counsel of His own will." Know that God has already seen the end result of the whole matter.

Daily Prayer

Father God, thank you for giving me the desire and ability to do what I have been called to do, in the Name of Jesus, Amen.

ASK AND RECEIVE

"Ask, and it shall be given you; seek, and ye shall find; knock, and it shall be opened unto you."

Matthew 7:7 (KJV)

There is never a need to beg the Father for anything; He knows what things we have need of before we ask Him. Death and life are in the power of the tongue, giving us power to decree things and they shall be established. Moreover, "A man's belly shall be satisfied with the fruits of his mouth; and with the increase of his lips shall he be filled." Yes, we are told to "ask, and it shall be given you; seek, and ye shall find; knock, and it shall be opened unto you: for everyone that asketh receiveth; and he that seeketh findeth; and to him that knocketh it shall be opened. For everyone that asketh receiveth; and he that seeketh findeth; and to him that knocketh it shall be opened." This is a promise; ask, seek, and knock today.

Daily Prayer

Father God, help me to always pray and ask for what I need according to your will, in the Name of Jesus, Amen.

KEPT BY THE WORD

"With my whole heart have I sought thee: O let me not wander from thy commandments."

Psalms 119:10 (KJV)

The Psalmist declared: "Thy Word is a lamp unto my feet, and a light unto my path." As believers, we can be confident that our steps are ordered in and by the Word of God. David declared: "Thy Word have I hidden in my heart that I my not sin against thee." It is by and through the Word of God that we are able to win the day, capture the promise, and walk through the attacks and distractions of the enemy. It is through the Word of God that we can command the events of the day and remain focused on what we have to do to fulfill our purpose on today. If we trust in the Lord with all our heart, He will direct our path. Trust Him.

Daily Prayer

Father God, help me to stay faithful to your Word that I may not offend you in anything that I do on today, in the Name of Jesus, Amen.

VICTORIOUS THROUGH CHRIST

"But thanks be to God, which giveth us the victory through our Lord Jesus Christ."

1 Corinthians 15:57 (KJV)

God has promised that we will be victorious through Christ Jesus, regardless of the enemy, the situation, or circumstance. The Word reminds us that we are more than conquerors through Christ Jesus. The Psalmist declared: "By this I know that thou favourest me, because mine enemy doth not triumph over me." We can do all things through Christ who strengthens us; this is a promise from the Father. God will enable you to be victorious today, regardless of how the day may have started out. God will come through for you at the appointed time. Always keep in mind that whatsoever is born of God overcomes! You are an overcomer.

Daily Prayer

Father God, thank you for always giving me the victory over my enemy, regardless of what it may involve, in the Name of Jesus, Amen.

HE IS OUR TRUST

"Some trust in chariots, and some in horses: but we will remember the Name of the Lord our God."

Psalms 20:7 (KJV)

The Lord is our trust. In Him we can depend and lean on at all times. He is able; He is faithful; He is forgiving; He is love; He is merciful; He is all-knowing; He is Omnipresent; He is all powerful; He is Lord of lords; He is King of kings; He is Alpha and Omega; He is our Father; and He loves us unconditionally. No matter the enemy, God is bigger. No matter the battle, He is our weapon. No matter the trial, He can see us through. We can safely trust in Him, regardless of the situation or circumstance. No matter what, if God be for us, who can be against us? The enemies will come, they will gather, they will plan; but know for a certainty that God did not send them. And, since He did not, they will not be able to prosper against you. Trust Him now.

Daily Prayer

Father God, I place all of my trust in you, and please let me never be ashamed before any of my enemies, in the Name of Jesus, Amen.

BLESSED WITH FAVOR

"For thou, Lord, wilt bless the righteous; with favour wilt thou compass him as with a shield."

Psalms 5:12 (KJV)

Regardless of the current situation, no matter the battle, remember that "greater is He that is in you, than he that is in the world." The enemy has no comeback for this. You are blessed and highly favored, and no weapon that is formed against you will prosper, not one! Your enemy cannot destroy what God has planned for you; he can't overcome the purpose that God has for your life; he cannot undo what God has already declared or done. God's favor is yours, and it is off limits you your enemy. It is God's gift to you, and it is not open to the dictates, attacks, or will of any of your enemies. Rejoice and be glad; today is in the hands of a God who has nothing but good thoughts of you. His favor is yours today – receive it now.

Daily Prayer

Father God, thank you for favoring me all day, allowing me to experience your unconditional love and presence all day, in Jesus' Name, Amen.

SURROUNDED BY HIS PRESENCE

"Let God arise, let His enemies be scattered: let them also that hate Him flee before Him."

Psalms 68:1 (KJV)

The Psalmist declared: "Because thou hast made the Lord, which is my refuge, even the most High, thy habitation; there shall no evil befall thee, neither shall any plague come nigh thy dwelling. For He shall give His angels charge over thee, to keep thee in all thy ways. They shall bear thee up in their hands, lest thou dash thy foot against a stone." We are covered by His presence at all times; we are never detached from His grace and mercy. According to scripture: "He delivereth me from mine enemies: yea, thou liftest me up above those that rise up against me: thou hast delivered me from the violent man." Rest assured in the promise that when the wicked, even our enemies and our foes, come upon us to eat up our flesh, they will stumble and fall.

Daily Prayer

Father God, thank you for being my strength, protector, and shield from all of my enemies, in the Name of Jesus, Amen.

GREATER THAN MY ENEMIES

"Though an host should encamp against me, my heart shall not fear: though war should rise against me, in this will I be confident."

Psalms 27:3 (KJV)

Rejoice today, for you are never at the mercy of anyone or anything but always sin the grace and favor of the Father. Apostle Paul declared: "We are troubled on every side, yet not distressed; we are perplexed, but not in despair; persecuted, but not forsaken; cast down, but not destroyed." It does not matter who is against you; God is greater. "When the enemy shall come in like a flood, the Spirit of the Lord shall lift up a standard against him." Also, "The young lions do lack, and suffer hunger: but they that seek the Lord shall not want any good thing." No matter what the enemy tries today, no weapon that is formed against you will prosper.

Daily Prayer

Father God, thank you for being my defense against all my enemies and foes and for never leaving me at their mercy, in the Name of Jesus, Amen.

HE IS GUIDING ME

"O Lord, I know that the way of man is not in himself: it is not in man that walketh to direct his steps."

Jeremiah 10:23 (KJV)

If we commit our ways unto the Lord, He has promised to bring them to pass. We can do all things through Christ who strengthens us. "The steps of a good man are ordered by the Lord: and he delighteth in his way." If we trust in the Lord with all our heart and lean not unto our own way of thinking, He has promised to direct our paths. No matter what we plan, it will only come to pass through Christ. Declare today as the Psalmist: "In thee, O Lord, do I put my trust: let me never be put to confusion." God is our source for all that we need, today and in the future. Trust Him today, knowing that He will make all things work together on your behalf.

Daily Prayer

Father God, thank you for all that you make happen for me and never allowing me to be alone, in the Name of Jesus, Amen.

HE IS ALWAYS FAITHFUL

"Let us hold fast the profession of our faith without wavering; (for He is faithful that promised)."

Hebrews 10:23 (KJV)

We will reap what we have sown. It's the law of the Kingdom, and man cannot change or block it. Apostle Paul declared: "Let us not be weary in well doing: for in due season, we will reap if we faint not." It's not if, but it's a matter of when God will cause increase to occur for you. When it is your due season, God will make all things work together for your good. It does not have to be your turn, He can make it your time. Know that it is not left up to others, for the Word of the Lord declares that God determines the time and the seasons for us, and He can change them whenever He chooses to. Keep being faithful to God, your call, and your purpose; and watch God do supernatural things on your behalf.

Daily Prayer

Father God, thank you for your faithfulness to me in every area of my life, never allowing me to be in lack, in the Name of Jesus, Amen.

HE IS OUR PROVIDER

"Behold the fowls of the air: for they sow not, neither do they reap, nor gather into barns; yet your heavenly Father feedeth them. Are ye not much better than they?"

Matthew 6:26 (KJV)

If God feeds the birds, causes the flowers to blossom, and makes the grass grow, how much more shall He take care of us? In fact, Matthew declared:

> And why take ye thought for raiment? Consider the lilies of the field, how they grow; they toil not, neither do they spin: and yet I say unto you, That even Solomon in all his glory was not arrayed like one of these. Wherefore, if God so clothe the grass of the field, which today is, and tomorrow is cast into the oven, shall He not much more clothe you, O ye of little faith. Therefore take no thought, saying, what shall we eat? Or, what shall we drink? Or, wherewithal shall we be clothed?

God will provide all your need unconditionally and with love.

Daily Prayer

Father God, thank you for always providing my daily bread and for making my way prosperous, in Jesus' Name, Amen.

FAITH TO SPEAK IT AS DONE

"We having the same spirit of faith, according as it is written, I believed, and therefore have I spoken; we also believe, therefore speak."

2 Corinthians 4:13 (KJV)

The Word declares that "death and life are in the power of the tongue"; therefore, we must be deliberate in what we regularly say. Job declared: "Thou shalt also decree a thing, and it shall be established unto thee: and the light shall shine upon thy ways." We should speak what we believe, and believe what we speak. Remember, "Out of the abundance of the heart, the mouth speaketh." Speak what you would like to have, believe what you are asking for, and receive it as done for you in the Name of Jesus. Believe today that nothing good will be withheld from you on today. Let your words today be spoken out of faith, believing that God will fulfill all of His promises to you.

Daily Prayer

Father God, help me to speak only words of faith today, knowing that you are able to do exceeding abundantly above all that I can ask or think, in Jesus' Name, Amen.

SOUND SPEECH

"The mouth of a righteous man is a well of life: but violence covereth the mouth of the wicked."

Proverbs 10:11 (KJV)

The Book of Titus declared: "In all things shewing thyself a pattern of good works: in doctrine shewing uncorruptness, gravity, sincerity, sound speech, that cannot be condemned; that he that is of the contrary part may be ashamed, having no evil thing to say of you." James encouraged us to be "swift to hear, slow to speak, slow to wrath." Our speech is only a reflection of what is in our heart, and therefore speech is a matter of the heart. The Gospel of Matthew declared: "For out of the abundance of the heart the mouth speaketh." Our words can either give life to our desire, or they can destroy them as well. Be watchful of every word today.

Daily Prayer

Father God, help me to bridle my tongue so that my speech will be pleasing to you and that I may edify those around me, in the Name of Jesus, Amen.

SATISFIED IN HIM

"The Lord is my strength and my shield; my heart trusted in Him, and I am helped: therefore my heart greatly rejoiceth; and with my song will I praise Him."

Psalms 28:7 (KJV)

The Lord is our hope, strength, light, way, and truth; we dwell safely in Him. "He has been a shelter for us, and a strong tower from the enemy." He is a Sun and Shield for us as believers and guides our way in His Word. The Psalmist reminds us that "The Lord is our light and our salvation; whom shall we fear? The Lord is the strength of our lives; of whom shall we be afraid?" His Name is a strong tower; the righteous run to it and are safe. The Prophet Isaiah testified: "Behold, God is my salvation; I will trust, and not be afraid: for the Lord JEHOVAH is my strength and my song; He also is become my salvation." You have no need to worry or fear today. God is your strength.

Daily Prayer

Father God, thank you for being my strength and my resting place throughout my day, in the Name of Jesus, Amen.

TRIED AND TRUE

"As for God, His way is perfect; the Word of the Lord is tried: He is a buckler to all them that trust in Him."

2 Samuel 22:31 (KJV)

We are kept by the Word, directed by the Word, led by the Word, and shown the way to the Father. Apostle Paul declared: "And that from a child thou hast know the holy scriptures, which are able to make thee wise unto salvation through faith which is in Christ Jesus. All scripture is given by inspiration of God, and is profitable for doctrine, for reproof, for correction, for instruction in righteousness. That the man of God may be perfect, thoroughly furnished unto all good works." Everything in your way now or what will come before you in the future will have given way to the power and authority of the Word of God. It is your anchor throughout the day.

Daily Prayer

Father God, lead me in the direction that you would have me to go on today, in the Name of Jesus, Amen.

HE WILL GO BEFORE US

"And the Lord drave out from before us all the people, even the Amorites which dwelt in the land: therefore will we also serve the Lord; for He is our God."

Joshua 24:18 (KJV)

Since we know that the Lord is for us, why should we even give thought to compromising our beliefs or positions or faith? God will go before us today, paving a way that we can successfully navigate throughout the day. Keep in mind that the awesome presence of The Lord is far more superior than the absence of those who decided they no longer want to be in our lives. The Psalmist reminds us that "the eye of the Lord is upon them that fear Him, upon them that hope in His mercy; to deliver their soul from death, and to keep them alive in famine. Our soul waiteth for the Lord: He is our help and our shield." He will go before you and will always be a present help in trouble.

Daily Prayer

Father God, thank you for always making a way for me and for never allowing me to face anything alone, in the Name of Jesus, Amen.

PRAISE BELONGS TO HIM

"Praise ye the Lord. O give thanks unto the Lord; for He is good: for His mercy endureth for ever."

Psalms 106:1 (KJV)

The Lord is good; His mercy endureth unto all generations. The Lord is our source for all that we have need of. We are encouraged to give thanks from a grateful heart to the One who is worthy, the Lord God. The Psalmist declared: "Unto thee, O God, do we give thanks: for that thy Name is near thy wondrous works declare." Yes, God is good, His mercy is everlasting, and His truth endureth unto all generations. Being thankful for what we already have is a great start on the path to future blessings. Ungratefulness is a receipt for stymied promotions. We have so much to be thankful for, for the goodness of God is indescribable. Praise Him today, for He is worthy of all our praise.

Daily Prayer

Father God, I praise you for your goodness and for all of the blessings that you make available to me each day, in the Name of Jesus, Amen.

GUARDED CONVERSATION

"Let your speech be alway with grace, seasoned with salt, that ye may know how ye ought to answer every man."

Colossians 4:6 (KJV)

Our conversation should edify the hearer, bring honor to the Father, and lift those whom we address. Remember, death and life are in the power of the tongue; therefore, we should be very careful how we speak to others. David declared: "Thy Word have I hidden in my heart that I might not sin against thee." We must do as Apostle Paul suggested: "Let our speech be always be filled with grace, delivered with love, in the appropriate moment and time." Solomon declared: "A man hath joy by the answer of his mouth: and a word spoken in due season, how good is it!" So, it's not just our words but the time in which we say them. Use discernment when speaking today. Be a blessing to others with your words.

Daily Prayer

Father God, help me to speak in a manner today that is pleasing unto you so that the hearers will be edified, in Jesus' Name, Amen.

WE HAVE OVERCOME THE WORLD

"Ye are of God, little children, and have overcome them: because greater is He that is in you, than he that is in the world."

1 John 4:4 (KJV)

Because of the finished work of Christ, we have already overcome our enemies. We have overcome by the blood of the Lamb and by the word of our testimonies. We can declare as Job did: "Behold, God is mighty, and despiseth not any: He is mighty in strength and wisdom." You can face today with your many testimonies, knowing that what God has done, He can certainly do again. You can declare as Solomon did: "The thing that hath been, it is that which shall be: and that which is done is that which shall be done: and there is no new thing under the sun." Use your faith and testimonies to prevail against what the enemy tries to trip you up with today.

Daily Prayer

Father God, thank you for always bring me out so that I can have a testimony in every area of my life, in the Name of Jesus, Amen.

UNDER HIS DIRECTIONS

"Man's goings are of the Lord; how can a man then understand his own way?"

Proverbs 20:24 (KJV)

God has determined our end from the beginning, and He is not making things up for us as we go along. We must allow the Holy Spirit to lead us each day, for He knows what's in the mind of God. Following the path that God has for us may not always be smooth, but if we stay on the path, we are sure to get to our appointed destination. God is always a present help and always directing us in the path of righteousness for His Name sake. We can declare as the Psalmist did: "Whither shall I go from thy Spirit? Or whiter shall I flee from thy presence? If I ascend up into heaven, thou art there: if I make my bed in hell, behold, thou art there." God will direct your steps today if you will acknowledge Him in all of your doings.

Daily Prayer

Father God, thank you for directing my steps on today, making sure that I reach my appointed place, in the Name of Jesus, Amen.

PLEASING COMMUNICATION

"A wholesome tongue is a tree of life: but perverseness therein is a breach in the spirit."

Proverbs 15:4 (KJV)

Our words do matter and can serve to make someone feel better or worse before engaging in communication with us. Since death and life are in the power of the tongue, we should make a concerted effort today to speak life to a troubled situation, a troubled family member, friend, church member, co-worker, or even a stranger. It just may make their day or at least make them see things in a much different light. It's a great day to speak life to "it," regardless of what "it" is. The Psalmist declared: "The mouth of the righteous speaketh wisdom, and his tongue talketh of judgement. The law of his God is in his heart; none of his steps shall slide." Speak life to it today.

Daily Prayer

Father God, help me to put a bridle on my tongue that I speak only that which gives life today, in the Name of Jesus, Amen.

LET GOD GET THE GLORY

"If ye be reproached for the Name of Christ, happy are ye; for the spirit of glory and of God resteth upon you: on their part He is evil spoken of, but on your part He is glorified."

1 Peter 4:14 (KJV)

Apostle Peter declared: "Beloved, think it not strange thing happened unto you: but rejoice, inasmuch as ye are partakers of Christ's sufferings; that, when His glory shall be revealed, ye may be glad also with exceeding joy." The greater the call, the greater the attacks. If you've been under some serious attacks, you have a serious call on your life. Embrace it, go all in with it, and don't give up for anything. God has graced you to go through the attacks and will be with you every step of the way. Whatever you go through, God is overseeing it that the glory may be revealed in your struggle. Yes, it's all for His glory. Be encouraged.

Daily Prayer

Father God,help me to walk in the things that you have planned for me, knowing that all that I endure is for your glory, in the Name of Jesus, Amen.

THE GREAT THINGS OF GOD

"Thy righteousness also, O God, is very high, who hast done great things: O God, who is like unto thee!"

Psalms 71:19 (KJV)

God does great things for His children because of His unconditional love for us. The Psalmist declared: "Many, O Lord my God, are thy wonderful works which thou hast done, and thy thoughts which are to us-ward: they cannot be reckoned up in order unto thee: if I would declare and speak of them, they are more than can be numbered." The Lord will do great things for you on today, and the enemy cannot stop or block them from coming to pass. Be happy today, expect God's best, and look for God's favor to be upon you all day. Rest assured that God has a plan and purpose for you to succeed and to know that permission from others is not necessary.

Daily Prayer

Father God, thank you for the multiple benefits that you have planned for me on today, all in the Name of Jesus, Amen.

SPIRITUAL INSIGHT

"While we look not at the things which are seen, but at the things which are not seen: for the things which are seen are temporal; but the things which are not seen are eternal."

2 Corinthians 4:18 (KJV)

To the natural eye, it may appear at times that things are not getting better. However, as born-again believers, we know that what's coming is better than what has been. Christ is the Good Shepherd and has come that we may have life and life more abundantly. Let's never believe the lie of the enemy but declare that our God is able to do exceeding abundantly above all that we can ask or think. Apostle Paul declared: "But as it is written, eye hath not seen, nor ear heard, neither have entered into the heart of man, the things which God hath prepared for them that love Him." We walk by faith and not by sight, depending upon the Holy Spirit to lead us. Trust Him today.

Daily Prayer

Father God, help me to walk by faith and not by what my natural eyes see, in the Name of Jesus, Amen.

THE LORD SHALL DELIVER

"And the Lord shall help them, and deliver them: He shall deliver them from the wicked, and save them, because they trust in Him."

Psalms 37:40 (KJV)

We do not have to fear or worry today. God is able to deliver us out of the traps, snares, and any holds of the enemy. The Psalmist declared: "Offer unto God thanksgiving; and pay thy vows unto the most High: and call upon me in the day of trouble: I will deliver thee, and thou shalt glorify me." In times of trouble, The Lord will make a way for us to overcome and prosper. King David said: "Because he hath set his love upon Me, therefore will I deliver him: I will set him on high, because he hath known My Name. He shall call upon Me, and I will answer him: I will be with him in trouble; I will deliver him, and honour him. With long life will I satisfy him, and shew him my salvation." This is your promise for today.

Daily Prayer

Father God, thank you in advance for your deliverance from all that may attempt to ensnare me on today, in the Name of Jesus, Amen.

PREORDAINED BLESSINGS

"Moreover whom He did predestinate, them He also called: and whom He called, them He also justified: and whom He justified, them He also glorified."

Romans 8:30 (KJV)

God chose us in Him before the foundations of the world and determined our end from the beginning. We did not choose Him, but He chose us, even before we had done anything good or bad. God will not leave it up to chance on things concerning us. In fact, Apostle Paul reminded us that it is "God that works in us to will and to do of His good pleasure." We can rest assured that no one or nothing can derail what God has purposed for our lives. If we follow the leading of the Holy Spirit and the Word, we are certain to arrive at our destination on time. As with the Prophet Jeremiah, God called and purposed our lives before He formed us in the womb. You nor your purpose were accidental. God knew what you would do beforehand. Trust Him today.

Daily Prayer

Father God, help me to walk in the preordained purpose and call that you have for my life, in the Name of Jesus, Amen.

SEEDTIME AND HARVEST

"While the earth remaineth, seedtime and harvest, and cold and heat, and summer and winter, and day and night shall not cease."

Genesis 8:22 (KJV)

God has given us seedtime and harvest so that we can enjoy the blessings on a daily basis. According to Apostle Paul, "Now He that ministereth seed to the sower both minister bread for your food, and multiply your seed sown, and increase the fruits of your righteousness." In other words, God will give us seed for bread and seed for sowing, remembering that we will reap what we sow. Keep in mind that the harvest comes after the seed has been put into the ground, watered, cared for, and given time to come up. Don't become weary in well doing, for in due season you will reap if you faint not. Sow as the Spirit leads you and watch God cause your harvest to come forth.

Daily Prayer

Father God, show me today what to sow and where to sow to achieve maximum benefit, in Jesus' Name, Amen.

A MERRY HEART

"A merry heart doeth good like a medicine: but a broken spirit drieth the bones."

Proverbs 17:22 (KJV)

This is the day that the Lord has made, let's rejoice and be glad in it. No matter what happened on yesterday or even last night, God has given you new mercies on today, for His mercies are new every morning. The scripture also reminds us that "weeping may endure for a night, but joy cometh in the morning." The enemy hates to see you happy, for He knows that the Joy of the Lord is your strength, and he will do all that he can to take away your joy. He hates it when you praise God and can't stand it when you trust God in spite of your situation or circumstances. Keep the enemy off balance; keep them hating, angry, and disgusted with you. Enjoy all the many benefits that God has provided you!

Daily Prayer

Father God, thank you for giving me joy and happiness that only you can today, in the Name of Jesus, Amen.

RESTING IN HIM

"But now the Lord my God hath given me rest on every side, so that there is neither adversary nor evil occurrent."

1 Kings 5:4 (KJV)

We can know that the Lord has favored us because our enemy has not triumphed over us. Though our enemy comes in like a flood, the Spirit of the Lord will lift up a standard against him. The enemy's weapons will not prosper against us, for the Lord shall go before us and prosper our ways. David declared: "For in the time of trouble He shall hide me in His pavilion: in the secret of His tabernacle shall He hide me; He shall set me up upon a rock. And now shall my head be lifted up above mine enemies round about me: therefore, will I offer in His tabernacle sacrifices of joy; I will sing, yea, I will sing praises unto the Lord." Rest is Christ's finished work.

Daily Prayer

Father God, thank you for not allowing my enemies to be victorious over me, in the Name of Jesus, Amen.

TRIUMPHANT THROUGH CHRIST

"Now thanks be unto God, which always causeth us to triumph in Christ, and maketh manifest the savour of His knowledge by us in every place."

2 Corinthians 2:14 (KJV)

The power of God is greater than your struggle, greater than any enemy, greater than the failures of your past; therefore, don't allow anything to make you focus on what did or did not happen and not be ready to receive what God is doing at the moment. God always causes us to triumph over the works of our enemies. Give God glory that the spirits that are against us are not as great as the Holy Spirit that is in us. You have the power over the enemy through Christ Jesus, regardless of what it is. Remember, "the weapons of our warfare are not carnal, but mighty through God to the pulling down of strongholds," and "no weapon that is formed against you will prosper." You are an overcomer.

Daily Prayer

Father God, thank you for causing me to be triumphant over my enemies today, in the Name of Jesus, Amen.

GOD-GIVEN PROSPERITY

"And I have given you a land for which ye did not labour, and cities which ye built not, and ye dwell in them; of the vineyards and oliveyards which ye planted not do ye eat."

Joshua 24:13 (KJV)

The Lord has promised to give us houses we did not build, vineyards we did not plant, and land in which we did not labor to own. The Gospel according to Matthew declared: "And everyone that hath forsaken houses, or brethren, or sisters, or father, or mother, or wife, or children, or lands, for My Name's sake, shall receive an hundredfold, and shall inherit everlasting life." It is the Father's pleasure to give you the Kingdom. It is in the Father's authority to give to us land, houses, and crops that are available to us; for "the earth is the Lord's and the fullness thereof, the world and they that dwell therein." The Gold and silver are His. Even the cattle on a thousand hills belong unto our God. Enjoy the benefits.

Daily Prayer

Father God, thank you for the daily benefits that you provide to me every day, in Jesus' Name, Amen.

LIFT HIM UP

"And I, if I be lifted up from the earth, will draw all men unto me."
John 12:32 (KJV)

We are God's workmanship, created in Christ Jesus unto good works, which God hath before ordained that we should walk in them." Apostle John declared: "Herein is the Father glorified, that ye bear much fruit; so shall ye be my disciples." We should remind the lost that they can be saved, the poor that poverty is not for them, the sick that they can be healed, and the blind that they can receive their sight. We are to help make disciples of men, lifting up the Name Jesus as we be witness to the saving grace of our Lord. If we lift Him up, it is Christ who will draw men unto Himself. Let's tell of the goodness of Jesus to someone today, and God will do the drawing.

Daily Prayer

Father God, help me to allow my light to shine today that men will see my light but glorify you, in Jesus' Name, Amen.

WALKING IN DIVINE AUTHORITY

"Then He called His twelve disciples together, and gave them power and authority over all devils, and to cure diseases."

Luke 9:1 (KJV)

God has not only given us power (ability) but also authority (right) over evil spirits. The Lord has empowered us to "tread upon serpents and scorpions, and over all the power of the enemy: and nothing shall by any means hurt you." We do not have the spirit of fear, for "God has not given us the spirit of fear, but of power, and of love, and of a sound mind." The enemy goes about as a roaring lion, but he has no power or authority over you. The Lord has given you the authority to decree a thing, and it shall be established. Don't allow the enemy to threaten you with anything today; he knows that He has no authority over you. Never fall for the trick.

Daily Prayer

Father God, help me to walk in the power and authority that you have given me on today, in the Name of Jesus, Amen.

THE LORD IS MY STRENGTH

"The Lord is my strength and my shield; my heart trusted in Him, and I am helped..."

Psalms 28:7 (KJV)

The Lord is the source for all that you will need. It is through Him that we live, move, and have our being. He is our strength, our peace, our shield, and our provider. We are never helpless, for we can do all things through Christ who strengthens us. It is not by power, nor by might, but by the Spirit that we overcome. As believers, we lift our eyes unto the hills from where all of our help comes. We learn to wait on the Lord, Knowing that when we do, we renew our strength and mount up with wings as eagles. We don't have to try to be strong in our own strength, but in His. We can overcome all that the enemy tries against us through Christ.

Daily Prayer

Father God, thank you for being my strength and a present help for me throughout the day, in the Name of Jesus, Amen.

ALL THINGS ARE POSSIBLE

"Jesus said unto him, If thou canst believe, all things are possible to him that believeth."

Mark 9:23 (KJV)

Jesus said that nothing is impossible to them that believe, and nothing is too hard for the Lord to do for His children. The Jesus declared:

> "For verily I say unto you, that whosoever shall say unto this mountain, be thou removed, and be thou cast into the sea; and shall not doubt in his heart, but shall believe that those things which he saith shall come to pass; he shall have whatsoever he saith. Therefore I say unto you, what things soever ye desire, when ye pray, believe that ye receive them, and ye shall have them."

As you go throughout the day, declare that I can do all things through Christ who strengthens me. Declare it now.

Daily Prayer

Father God, thank you for making all things possible through Christ for me on today, in the Name of Jesus, Amen.

MADE ME VICTORIOUS

"He delivered me from my strong enemy, and from them that hated me: for they were too strong for me."

2 Samuel 22:18 (KJV)

It is God who caused us to win; it is through Christ that we overcame the enemy; it is because of Christ that we became conquerors. It's not who is against us but that God is for us. It's not about what's impossible but that with God, all things are possible. It's never the size of the enemy but the fact that greater is He that is within us than he that is in the world. In fact, "if God is for us, who really can be against us?" The way may not be easy, but if it's of God, it will withstand the test. We are told to "think it not strange concerning the fiery trial which is to try you, as though some strange thing happened to you." This is not a one-time deal; these are your rights and promises each and every single day. Enjoy.

Daily Prayer

Father God, thank you for delivering me from the hand of my enemies and not allowing me to fall prey to any of them, in Jesus' Name, Amen.

HEAVENLY THOUGHTS

"How precious also are thy thoughts unto me, O God! How great is the sum of them!"

Psalms 139:17 (KJV)

You are in the thoughts of God, and they are too numerous to number. Remember that the Prophet Jeremiah declared of the Lord: "For I know the thoughts that I think toward you, thoughts of peace, and not of evil to bring you unto an expected end." God's plans are not debatable, for He will complete all that concerns you. You can rest assured that He is watching over you, overseeing your activities and directing you through the Holy Spirit to make sure that you complete what He has planned for you on today. Allow the Holy Spirit to continue leading you; He is the comforter sent along to comfort, teach, and guide you. Follow His lead today.

Daily Prayer

Father God, thank you for keeping me in mind, leading me, guiding me, and directing me throughout the day, in the Name of Jesus, Amen.

SOLID FOUNDATION

"And the rain descended, and the floods came, and the winds blew, and beat upon that house; and it fell not: for it was founded upon a rock."
Matthew 7:25 (KJV)

Christ is the Rock on which we stand; all else is like sinking sand. He is the Rock in a weary land, a shelter in the time of storms, a leaning post for those who are tired from the journey. When you are standing on a firm foundation, all the drama in the world can't shake your faith or belief. Come what may, know that Christ is not moving or going anywhere, for He is always a present help. The King David declared: "The Lord is my rock, and my fortress, and my deliverer; my God, my strength, in whom I will trust; my buckler, and the horn of my salvation, and my high tower." The Word further declared: "They that trust in the Lord shall be as mount Zion, which abides forever and shall not be removed." Stay on the Rock.

Daily Prayer

Father God, it is you that I stand upon day and night; for you are my strength and source for all I need, in the Name of Jesus, Amen.

GOD WILL MAKE IT HAPPEN

"Shall I bring to the birth, and not cause to bring forth? saith the Lord: shall I cause to bring forth, and shut the womb? saith thy God."

Isaiah 66:9 (KJV)

Whatever God has purposed cannot be denied, stopped, or derailed. The Prophet Isaiah declared: "This is the purpose that is purposed upon the whole earth: and this is the hand that is stretched out upon all the nations. For the Lord of host hath purposed, and who shall disannul it? And His hand is stretched out, and who shall turn it back?" God will not give you a call, purpose, or a promise and not make it good or fulfill it. Be reminded also that "whatsoever born of God overcometh the world: and this is the victory that overcometh the world, even our faith." God is not going to get you to the door and shut it nor bring you to the brink of victory and not allow you to win. Trust Him today.

Daily Prayer

Father God, thank you for working in me to will and to do of your good pleasure, in the Name of Jesus, Amen.

POWER OF YOUR WORDS

"The mouth of a righteous man is a well of life: but violence covereth the mouth of the wicked."

Proverbs 10:11 (KJV)

Death and life are in the power of the tongue; therefore, we have been given the authority to speak those things that be not as though they were. Solomon declared: "A man's belly shall be satisfied with the fruit of his mouth; and with the increase of his lips shall he be filled." Life is in the power of the righteous; speak life today, all day, over every situation or circumstance. Job reminds us that "we can decree and thing, and it shall be established unto us: and the light shall shine upon our ways." Don't fear. We are the righteousness of God through Christ Jesus. The Psalmist declared: "The mouth of the righteous speaketh wisdom, and his tongue talketh of judgement." All day, speak words of life, hope, and joy to all that concerns you.

Daily Prayer

Father God, help me to guard my mouth that I do not utter anything that is harmful to those that I encounter today, in the Name of Jesus, Amen.

IN GOOD HANDS

"Though he fall, he shall not be utterly cast down: for the Lord upholdeth him with his hand."

Psalms 37:24 (KJV)

You can rest assured today that come what may, you are in the hands of God, and no one is able to pluck you out of them. The Lord has given His angels charge over you to keep you in all of your ways that you do not dash your feet against the stone. The Psalmist declared: "Surely He shall deliver thee from the snare of the fowler, and from the noisome pestilence. He shall cover thee with His feathers, and under His wings shalt thou trust: His truth shall be thy shield and buckler. Thou shalt not be afraid for the terror by night; nor for the arrow thy flieth by day." Also, "A just man falleth seven times, but gets back up again." You are in good hands today.

Daily Prayer

Father God, thank you for covering me all day and for holding me in thy hands that I am not overcome by my enemy, in the Name of Jesus, Amen.

BLESSINGS FLOW FROM HIM

"The Lord hath been mindful of us: He will bless us; He will bless the house of Israel; He will bless the house of Aaron."

Psalms 115:12 (KJV)

Every good gift and every perfect gift is from above, and cometh down from the Father of lights, with whom is no variableness, neither shadow of turning." In other words, all that is good is because of and through the Lord God. The blessings of the Lord maketh rich and causes no sorrow with it. You don't have to worry; it does not grieve God to bless you. In fact, Apostle John declared: "Beloved, I wish above all things that thou mayest prosper and be in health, even as thy soul prospereth." King Solomon declared: "A faithful man shall abound in blessings: but he that maketh haste to be rich shall not be innocent." The Lord is blessing you right now – enjoy it.

Daily Prayer

Father God, thank you for the many blessings that I have been given, and thank you for always watching over me each day, in the Name of Jesus, Amen.

ESTABLISHED BY THE LORD

"He brought me up also out of an horrible pit, out of the miry clay, and set my feet upon a rock, and established my goings."

Psalms 40:2 (KJV)

It is the Lord who delivered us, and it is He who has kept us from all hurt, harm, and danger. "It is God that girdeth me with strength, and maketh my way perfect. He has made our feet like hinds' feet, and setteth me upon my high places." We are made steady, strong, and firm through Jesus Christ. The Psalmist declared: "And let the beauty of the Lord our God be upon us: and establish thou the work of our hands upon us; yea, the work of our hands establish thou it." We do not have to worry about the wind or storm, for the Lord has established us in the earth. Trust Him today.

Daily Prayer

Father God, thank you for placing my feet on a solid foundation and establishing my goings and comings, in the Name of Jesus, Amen.

LIKE HIM

"For thou hast made him a little lower than the angels, and hast crowned him with glory and honor. Thou madest him to have dominion over the works of thy hands; thou hast put all things under his feet."

Psalms 8:5-6 (KJV)

No matter what the enemy tries to say to us or about us, he can never change how we have been created by the Lord. The prophet Zechariah stated: "For thus saith the Lord of hosts; after the glory hath He sent me unto the nations which spoiled you: for he that toucheth you toucheth the apple of His eye." What a testimony to what the Lord said about us and how He feels about us. He has made us just a little lower than angels and crowned us with His glory and honor. He placed us over all the works of His hand and gave us dominion over everything that He created. Today, we can rejoice for we are His workmanship, created unto Him for good works. We are blessed and highly favored.

Daily Prayer

Father God, thank you for making me the apple of your eye and never leaving me alone, in Jesus' Name, Amen.

THE RIGHT DIRECTION

"And the Lord direct your hearts into the love of God, and into the patient waiting for Christ."

2 Thessalonians 3:5 (KJV)

It is God who works within us to will and to do His pleasure. With Him we can do all things; however, without Him we can do absolutely nothing. We are told to "trust in the Lord with all our heart, and lean not unto our own understanding; in all our ways acknowledge Him and He will direct our path." He can only do this if we are sensitive to the leading of the Holy Spirit and spend quality time in His Word. "The steps of a good man are ordered by the Lord," and he delighteth in His way. There is no need to be fearful; the Lord, through the Holy Spirit, will lead us unto all truth. Follow Him today.

Daily Prayer

Father God, help me to walk according to the leading of the Holy Spirit today that I do not go astray, in the Name of Jesus, Amen.

HE REVIVES ME

"My flesh and my heart faileth: but God is the strength of my heart, and my portion for ever."

Psalms 73:26 (KJV)

King David declared: "The Lord is my Shepherd; I shall not want. He maketh me to lie down in green pastures: He leadeth me beside the still waters." No matter where we may find ourselves, God can and will revive us. His mercy is everlasting, and His truth endureth unto all generations. He will restore every area in which we may have become weak. We should declare today as the Psalmist did: "Though I walk in the midst of trouble, thou wilt revive me: thou shalt stretch forth thine hand against the wrath of mine enemies, and thy right hand shall save me." The Lord will restore all that we turn over to Him. Trust Him for restoration and comfort today.

Daily Prayer

Father God, thank you for being my strength and for always lifting me out of all my troubles, in the Name of Jesus, Amen.

GREATER IS COMING

"The glory of this latter house shall be greater than of the former, saith the Lord of hosts…"

Haggai 2:9 (KJV)

The Lord has promised that our ending will be greater than our beginning, regardless of what we may have experienced or are currently experiencing. This is further illustrated in the Book of Isaiah: "Declaring the end from the beginning, and from ancient times the things that are not yet done, saying, My counsel shall stand, and I will do all my pleasure." And, since God has planned it, who will be able to turn it back. We must remind ourselves that if He did something before, He can certainly do it again; for He is the same yesterday, today, and forever. The Glory of the latter house will be greater than the former; expect greater to come.

Daily Prayer

Father God, thank you for prearranging my future outcome and destination, in the Name of Jesus, Amen.

GODLY ASSURANCE

"For the Lord God will help me; therefore shall I not be confounded: therefore have I set my face like a flint, and I know that I shall not be ashamed."

Isaiah 50:7 (KJV)

We never have to worry about being alone or being without assistance. The Lord will help us through the Holy Spirit. John declared: "But the Comforter, which is the Holy Ghost, whom the Father will send in my name, He shall teach you all things, and bring all things to your remembrance, whatsoever I have said unto you." We all should decree as Isaiah did: "Behold the Lord God will help me; who is he that condemn me? Lo, they all shall wax old as a garment; the moth shall eat them up." Regardless of the need, situation, or condition, we do not have to fear; the help will be there. His presence will be with us all day, wherever we may find ourselves.

Daily Prayer

Father God, thank you for being my present help, not just in time of troubles, but always, in the Name of Jesus, Amen.

HE IS FIGHTING FOR US

"For the Lord your God is He that goeth with you, to fight for you against your enemies, to save you."

Deuteronomy 20:4 (KJV)

Regardless of the enemy, no matter the battle, whoever or whatever may be against us, God is fighting for us and is greater than anything that is against us. Regardless of the next move of our enemies, God already knows what He will do through us and for us. The outcome of our battles, conflicts, or encounters are not left to chance. The weapons won't work against us. We can claim it; declare it. "When the enemy shall come in like a flood, the Spirit of the Lord shall lift up a standard against him." Apostle Paul declared: "Now thanks be unto God, which always causeth us to triumph in Christ, and maketh manifest the savour of His knowledge by us in every place." Yes, He is fighting for us!

Daily Prayer

Father God, thank you for always fighting for me and for always causing me to triumph over my enemies, in the Name of Jesus, Amen.

COVERED BY GRACE TODAY

"Let us therefore come boldly unto the throne of grace, that we may obtain mercy, and find grace to help in time of need."

Hebrews 4:16 (KJV)

No matter the situation, grace is always available to the believer. This amazing gift cannot be earned or purchased; it can only be received by faith. Nothing can compete with it, compare to it, or overcome it. Why is this? Because Christ is the "Grace" of God. If you have Christ, you have Grace – they are inseparable! It is by grace that you are saved; it is because of grace that your sins are forgiven; it is by grace that you can receive the blessings of Abraham in your life. Yes, you can go boldly to the throne of Grace and obtain mercy and find grace to help in time of need today. You don't have to pay for it today, hope for it, or look for it; it is a free gift from the Father.

Daily Prayer

Father God, thank you for grace and all of its benefits that it has made available for me on today, in the Name of Jesus, Amen.

OUR HIDING PLACE

"For in the time of trouble He shall hide me in His pavilion: in the secret of His tabernacle shall He hide me; He shall set me up upon a rock."

Psalms 27:5 (KJV)

God has promised to never leave or forsake you. No matter the seriousness of the issue or situation, God will be a present help for you. He is your present help – never late, never too early, never out of season. The Psalmist declared: "In my distress [when I seemed surrounded] I called upon the Name of the Lord and cried to my God for help; He heard my voice from His temple, and my cry for help came before Him, into His very ears." You can be assured that God will be a shelter for you, a strong tower, a hiding place, and a shield from the storms and any enemy. The Lord is your keeper, and "He shall cover thee with His feathers, and under His wings shalt thou trust: His truth shall be thy shield and buckler." You will be protected today.

Daily Prayer

Father God, thank you for being my hiding place and my protection for all that would do me harm, in the Name of Jesus, Amen.

GOD'S PLANS WILL STAND

"The counsel of the Lord standeth for ever, the thoughts of His heart to all generations."

Psalms 33:11 (KJV)

God worketh all things after the counsel of His own will. Nothing is or will be left to chance concerning your current status or in the future. God's purpose is unchangeable; therefore, regardless of the attempts of your enemy, your purpose in life will not change. No matter what the day holds, God is not threatened by any of it. Whatever God purposes, it will happen when He wills it, how He wills it, and where He wills it to happen. Because you love God and are the called according to His purpose, God has promised to make all things work together for your good. Apostle Paul reminds us that "we have obtained an inheritance, being predestinated according to the purpose of Him who worketh all things after the counsel of His own will." His purpose will be fulfilled in you today.

Daily Prayer

Father God, thank you for including me in your plans, plans that will bring you glory, in the Name of Jesus, Amen.

EVERYTHING IN HIM

"My goodness, and my fortress; my high tower, and my deliverer; my shield, and He in whom I trust; who subdueth my people under me."

Psalms 144:2 (KJV)

What we face today will not define us; it's what we do that will. As we navigate through the hurdles and distractions of the day, we must keep in mind that we have God's assurance of peace, protection, guidance, and provisions. Nothing we will face today will be bigger than God's grace, nothing stronger than His mercy, nothing greater than His unconditional love for us. We are the apple of God's eye, and nothing can pluck us out of His hands. We can declare as the Psalmist did: "The Lord is my rock, and my fortress, and my deliverer; my God, my strength, in whom I will trust; my buckler, and the horn of my salvation." It is all because of and through Christ; trust Him for all that you need on today.

Daily Prayer

Father God, thank you for being my fortress from the battle and my deliverer from all that had me trapped, in Jesus, Amen.

LOOKING UNTO HIM

"My voice shalt thou hear in the morning, O Lord; in the morning will I direct my prayer unto thee, and will look up."

Psalms 5:3 (KJV)

If you are struggling with a decision today, experiencing a major disappointment, or dealing with a personal loss, please know that God's comforting Spirit will be there for you, helping you through these difficult times. God is your source for all that you will need today; never allow the enemy to make you feel that God is not with you or for you. Keep looking unto Jesus, the Author and finisher of your faith; and you will be able to overcome the attacks of your enemy, the personal struggles you may face, and the battles that you will engage in during the day. The Lord is your refuge and strength, a very present help in trouble. He will never forsake or leave you. Trust in Him today, cast all your cares upon Him and leave them there.

Daily Prayer

Father God, thank you for being my help and my comfort throughout all of my trials and troubles, in Jesus' Name, Amen.

JOY IN HIM

"Therefore with joy shall ye draw water out of the wells of salvation."
Isaiah 12:3 (KJV)

The Joy of the Lord is your strength. The Lord will give you joy as you draw near unto Him, blessing you with His presence to keep you encouraged and lifted. The scripture declared: "They that sow in tears shall reap in joy. He that goeth forth and weepeth, bearing precious seed, shall doubtless come again with rejoicing, bringing his sheaves with him." Even through your tears, keep moving forward; in the midst of troubles, continue to trust God; in your darkest hours, continue to look to the hills from whence your help comes – all the while knowing that "weeping may endure for a night, but joy comes in the morning." It is not your strength but His strength that will see you through. Stay strong in the Lord.

Daily Prayer

Father God, thank you for flooding my soul with joy today, joy like a river, in the Name of Jesus, Amen.

BE ON GUARD TODAY

"Keep thy heart with all diligence; for out of it are the issues of life."
Proverbs 4:23 (KJV)

The enemy will do all he can today to get you to speak words that do not edify or build you or others up. To the best of your ability, keep out of your mind or thoughts everyone and everything that make you think negatively, speak negatively, or doubt what you know to be truth. Remember, as a man thinks in his heart, so is he; therefore, you cannot allow what you don't want to come out of your mouth to enter into your mind. Apostle Paul declared: "Let no corrupt communication proceed out of your mouth, but that which is good to the use of edifying, that it may minister grace unto the hearers." Be diligent to speak the Word today; it will bring great benefits.

Daily Prayer

Father God, help me to guard my heart and mind that nothing negative or destructive may come to me, in the Name of Jesus, Amen.

HE ALWAYS KEEPS HIS WORD

"That confirmeth the word of His servant, and performeth the counsel of His messengers..."

Isaiah 44:26 (KJV)

God will always keep His Word. He will never go against His Word, for scripture declared: "God is not a man, that He should lie; neither the son of man, that He should repent: hath He said, and shall He not do it? Or hath He spoken, and shall He not make it good?" God watches over His Word to perform it; therefore, you can be assured that not one of His promises will fail. Trust in the Lord with all your heart, and believe that what was promised to you will come to pass. The Prophet Samuel declared: "As for God, His way is perfect; the word of the Lord is tried: He is a buckler to all them that trust in Him." You can rest assured that the Word still works. Trust it and Him today.

Daily Prayer

Father God, thank you for always keeping your word and for performing all that you promised me, in Jesus' Name, Amen.

GOD DID IT FOR ME

"I sought the Lord, and He heard me, and delivered me from all my fears."
Psalms 34:4 (KJV)

When feeling alone, know that you are not; when feeling over-whelmed, know that you have help in Jesus Christ. You can go bold-ly to the throne of grace to obtain mercy and find grace to help in the time of need. Declare today as the Psalmist did: "From the end of the earth will I cry unto thee, when my heart is overwhelmed: lead me to the rock that is higher than I." Know that God will never forsake nor leave you, regardless of your current situation or condi-tion. You can say as David did: "He brought me forth also into a large place: He delivered me, because He delighted in me." The Lord will deliver you; trust Him with all your concerns and issues today.

Daily Prayer

Father God, thank you for being my deliverer and my strong tower that I can go to each day, in the Name of Jesus, Amen.

THE LORD DID THIS

"Because he hath set his love upon me, therefore, will I deliver him: I will set him on high, because he hath known my Name."

Psalms 91:14 (KJV)

Regardless of your past, regardless of what did or not happen on yesterday, regardless of your current status, God is your deliverer. Your past cannot affect your future if you follow the leading of the Holy Spirit and allow Him to direct you. King David declared: "I've been young and now am old; yet have I not seen the righteous forsaken nor his seed begging bread." You do not have to fear, worry, or be in doubt. God is "able to do exceeding abundantly above all that you can ask or think according to the power that works in you." God is for you; trust Him to direct your steps so that you can achieve what He has planned for you today.

Daily Prayer

Father God, thank you for keeping me through all of my situations and circumstances, making me victorious over my enemies today, in Jesus' Name, Amen.

IT WILL TURN IN YOUR FAVOR

"The meek also shall increase their joy in the Lord, and the poor among men shall rejoice in the Holy One of Israel."

Isaiah 29:19 (KJV)

God will turn "it" around in your favor, and nothing you have done or the enemy tries to do can stop Him from favoring you on today. Believe now that God will make more available to you than what was available in the past. Believe now that God's finished work does not need man's approval to operate in your life. Declare today as the Psalmist did: "Blessed be the Lord, who daily loadeth us with benefits, even the God of our salvation." Believe today that "The Lord shall increase you more and more, you and your seed. Yea, the Lord shall give that which is good; and our land shall yield her increase." God will not do less but more for you; decree that abundance is for you and that you will receive all that God has purposed for you on today.

Daily Prayer

Father God, thank you for favoring me with increase in every area of my life on today, in the Name of Jesus, Amen.

THE FATHER WILL LIFT ME

"When men are cast down, then thou shalt say, There is lifting up; and He shall save the humble person."

Job 22:29 (KJV)

Christ is able to lift the bowed down head, the weary soul, and the troubled spirit. The Psalmist declared: "Lift up your heads, O ye gates; and be ye lift up, ye everlasting doors; and the King of Glory shall come in. Who is this King of glory? The Lord strong and mighty, the Lord mighty in battle." Also, "The Lord upholdeth all that fall, and raiseth up all those what be bowed down. The Lord openeth the eyes of the blind: the Lord raiseth them that are bowed down: the Lord loveth the righteous." Have no fears today, for if the enemy comes out against you like a flood, the Lord will lift up a standard against him. He has you covered.

Daily Prayer

Father God, when my heart is overwhelmed, please lead me to the Rock that is higher than I am, in Jesus' Name, Amen.

SOW IT TODAY

"Cast thy bread upon the waters: for thou shalt find it after many days."
Ecclesiastes 11:1 (KJV)

Don't allow the current situation or position prevent you from following through with what you have purposed to do. The conditions may not be perfect; however, it just may be the right time to pursue the particular endeavor. Solomon declared: "As thou knowest not what is the way of the spirit, nor how the bones do grow in the womb of her that is with child: even so thou knowest not the works of God who maketh all. In the morning sow thy seed, and in the evening withhold not thine hand: for thou knoweth not whether shall prosper, either this or that, or whether they both shall be alike good." Look for opportunities to give and grow today; God is with you.

Daily Prayer

Father God, help me to discern the times and seasons so that I will not be slack in sowing into the lives of others, in the Name of Jesus, Amen.

THE SOLID ROCK

"He is the Rock, His work is perfect: for all His ways are judgment: a God of truth and without iniquity, just and right is He."

Deuteronomy 32:4 (KJV)

You can be assured that God will not change on you; for He is the same yesterday, today, and forever. He is the solid Rock on which you can stand today, knowing that in Him you will not be moved. The psalmist declared: "Be thou my strong habitation, whereunto I may continually resort: thou hast given commandment to save me; for thou art my rock and my fortress." He will be there for you today, protecting you, leading you, guiding you, caring for you, and interceding for you as you go throughout the day. Rest assured that the day will not present you anything that God's grace will not empower you to overcome, regardless of what it is. He is the Rock upon which you can always stand firm.

Daily Prayer

Father God, thank you for your presence and for always keeping me and providing for me, in the Name of Jesus, Amen.

EVERYTHING AFTER ITS KIND

"And God said, Let the earth bring forth grass, the herb yielding seed, and the fruit tree yielding fruit after his kind, whose seed is in itself, upon the earth: and it was so."

Genesis 1:11 (KJV)

Our surroundings will affect every aspect of our lives, good and bad. Therefore, we must be mindful to what we join ourselves. We are told to "mark the perfect man, and behold the upright: for the end of that man is peace. But the transgressors shall be destroyed together: the end of the wicked shall be cut off. But salvation of the righteousness is of the Lord: He is their strength in the time of trouble." Everything reproduces after its kind; therefore, it is imperative that we be careful what and who we join ourselves to, for we could be reproducing the kind of behavior and acts of our surroundings. We really can become the products of our environments. Ask God for godly discernment for all that you are or will become a part of.

Daily Prayer

Father God, help me to be mindful of those around me and all of my surroundings so that I will not be negatively affected by them, in the Name of Jesus, Amen.

THEY THAT SEEK HIM WILL

"And they that know thy name will put their trust in thee: for thou, Lord, hast not forsaken them that seek thee."

Psalms 9:10 (KJV)

Regardless of the plans of the enemy, we can rest assured that God will be there for us: guiding, fighting, shielding, and protecting us. We can know that the righteous will never be forsaken, nor will his seed ever have to beg for food. Through Christ, we can do all things; through Him we will make it. His power exceeds; His love is unconditional; His mercy is everlasting; and His grace is sufficient. The scripture reminds us that "Ye are of God, little children, and have overcome them: because greater is He that is in you, than he that is in the world." God will not allow the weapons of the enemy to prosper against us. Declare today as King David did: "I will say of the Lord, He is my refuge and my fortress: my God; in Him will I trust."

Daily Prayer

Father God, thank you for never forsaking me, never forgetting about me, and never allowing me to walk alone, in Jesus' Name, Amen.

FULLY COMMITTED TO THE TASK

"Whatsoever thy hand findeth to do, do it with thy might; for there is no work, nor device, nor knowledge, nor wisdom, in the grave, whither thou goest."

Ecclesiastes 9:10 (KJV)

Whatever you do on today, do it as unto the Lord, knowing that "the faithful shall abound in blessings." This is the day that the Lord has made, and it's an excellent opportunity to do something awesome. Make the day count; excuses are never an alternative. Solomon declared: "Seest thou a man diligent in his business? He shall stand before kings; he shall not stand before mean men." The Gospel according to Luke declared: "He that is faithful in that which is least is faithful also in much: and he that is unjust in the least is unjust also in much." Yes, with all that is within you, do everything today with all strength, will, and power that you possess.

Daily Prayer

Father God, help me to serve you through others with all my abilities, in the Name of Jesus, Amen.

FAITH WITHOUT WORKS DOESN'T WORK

"Seeth thou how faith wrought with his works, and by works was faith made perfect?"

James 2:22 (KJV)

James clearly describes that faith without works is dead, being unfruitful and of none effect. For as the body without the spirit is dead, so is faith without works. No matter how badly we want something to change, if we do not work and do something, our intentions will never materialize. James further stated: "What doth it profit, my brethren, though a man say he hath faith, and have not works? Can faith save him? Moreover, yea, a man may say, Thou hast faith, and I have works: shew me thy faith without thy works, and I will shew thee my faith by my works." We must put hands and feet to our faith and decree "things that be not as though they were" and do what is required to put our faith into action.

Daily Prayer

Father God, help me to put my faith into action, knowing that professed faith is useless without works, in the Name of Jesus, Amen.

WE HAVE THE MERCY OF THE LORD

"Which in time past were not a people, but are now the people of God: which had not obtained mercy, but now have obtained mercy."

1 Peter 2:10 (KJV)

One of the many benefits that God daily bestows upon us is His abundant mercy. This mercy is everlasting and is granted without request. King David declared: "Surely goodness and mercy shall follow me all the days of my life." What a promise; what an assurance. The Lord is a God of mercy, for "Thou, Lord, art good, and ready to forgive; and plenteous in mercy unto all them that call upon thee." He is full of "compassion, and gracious, longsuffering, and plenteous in mercy and truth." God is good, His mercy is everlasting, and His truth endureth unto all generations. No matter what today offers, you can rest assured that God's mercy will be greater.

Daily Prayer

Father God, thank you for your awesome mercy that you daily send my way, protecting me, caring for me, and meeting all my needs, in the Name of Jesus, Amen.

HOPE OF MY LIFE

"Now the God of hope fill you will all joy and peace in believing, that ye may abound in hope, through the power of the Holy Ghost."

Romans 15:13 (KJV)

It is said that hope makes the heart glad, and it can be further said that without hope, life can be unfulfilling or barren. King Solomon declared: "Hope deferred maketh the heart sick: but when the desire cometh, it is a tree of life." Regardless of the situation or circumstance on today, try to the best of your ability to do as Abraham did: "Who against hope believed in hope, that he might become the father of many nations; according to that which was spoken, so shall thy seed be." Abraham believed in Hope, though there was no human reason to believe; and because of this hope, he received the promise of the Lord. The Lord will do the same for you today if you keep your hope active.

Daily Prayer

Father God, my hope is in you; please never let me be without this hope, in the Name of Jesus, Amen.

RIGHTEOUS BY FAITH IN HIM

"For therein is the righteousness of God revealed from faith to faith: as it is written, The just shall live by faith."

Romans 1:17 (KJV)

Through faith, we understand that we have been made righteous. Through this knowledge, we can know that we are the righteousness of God through Christ Jesus. We are not becoming righteous, but we have been made righteous by the finished work of Christ. God made Jesus to be sin, who knew no sin, that we might become the righteousness of God through Christ Jesus. Furthermore, Apostle Paul declared: "Therefore being justified by faith, we have peace with God through our Lord Jesus Christ. By whom also we have access by faith into this grace wherein we stand, and rejoice in hope of the glory of God." We live by faith. Let this faith reassure you of your righteousness through Christ today.

Daily Prayer

Father God, thank you for seeing me as righteous through the blood of Christ, in His Name, Amen.

THERE IS NO OTHER GOD

"But the Lord is the true God, He is the living God, and an everlasting king..."

Jeremiah 10:10 (KJV)

To us, as believers there is No God like unto JEHOVAH! The Psalmist declared: "That men may know that thou, whose name alone is JEHOVAH, art the most high over all the earth." He is God and besides Him there is no other. The Prophet Isaiah declared: "Behold, God is my salvation; I will trust, and not be afraid: for the Lord JEHOVAH is my strength and my song; He also is become my salvation." Our Lord God is the King of kings, Lord of lords, Alpha and Omega, the beginning and the end. Knowing all of this, who can be against us?! Regardless of the situations or circumstances that may arise on today, nothing can be too great for our God.

Daily Prayer

Father God, thank you for being greater than anything that I will face on today, and I can safely rest in your protection, in Jesus' Name, Amen.

OUR TRUE HELPER

"For the Lord will not forsake His people for His great name's sake: because it hath pleased the Lord to make you His people."

1 Samuel 12:22 (KJV)

We are His people, the apple of His eye, and no one can pluck us out of His hands. We will never be forsaken or forgotten, regardless of what we do or don't do. Doesn't matter how much we love God and others. No matter how spiritual we think we are, difficult times will happen to all of us. However, we must remember that He is the same God before, during, and at the end of every situation. Praise God through it all. God is always a present help and a strong tower! Thank God that in troubled times, we will find comfort in Christ. With broken and sad hearts, we will yet praise the God of our salvation. Know that the Lord will not cast off His people. Neither will He forsake His heritage.

Daily Prayer

Father God, thank you for never leaving me alone and never forsaking me, in the Name of Jesus, Amen.

NOT FIGHTING ALONE

"For the Lord your God is He that goeth with you, to fight for you against your enemies, to save you."

Deuteronomy 20:4 (KJV)

We will never have to fight against the enemy alone, and regardless of the size or ability of the enemy, God will always be greater. God will fight for us at all times, in all places, and for all reasons. We do not have to fear, for greater is He that is in us than he that is in the world. Jeremiah declared: "Thou art my battle axe and weapons of war: for with thee will I break in pieces the nations, and with thee will I destroy kingdoms; and with thee will I break in pieces the horses and his riders; and with thee will I break in pieces the chariot and his rider." Yes, throughout the day, the Lord will go before you, fighting on your behalf so that you can have a successful day. All you need to do is be sensitive to the leading of His Spirit and obey.

Daily Prayer

Father God, thank you for leading me, going before me, and fighting for me throughout the day, in the Name of Jesus, Amen.

HE DOES NEW THINGS,
YET HE REMAINS THE SAME

"Behold, I will do a new thing; now it shall spring forth; shall ye not know it?"

Isaiah 43:19 (KJV)

Though He is the same yesterday, today, and forever, God does do new things for His people. His mercies are new every morning, regardless of what you may have experienced on the day before. The Prophet Isaiah declared: "Remember ye not the former things, neither consider the things of old. Behold, I will do a new thing; now it shall spring forth; shall ye not know it? I will even make a way in the wilderness, and rivers in the desert." Whatever has to be done, it is not too difficult for the Lord our God. He can even change the times and the seasons, if necessary, for you to be successful. Trust Him today for new vision, new revelation, and new anointings.

Daily Prayer

Father God, thank you for always doing new things for me and always keeping me ahead of my enemies, in the Name of Jesus, Amen.

HE WILL BRING ALL TO COMPLETION

"The Lord will perfect that which concerneth me…"

Psalms 138:8 (KJV)

You have gotta believe that what God has started, He will complete. Nothing will be missing, and nothing will be lacking. All that God has promised you on today will be fulfilled; believe nothing less will happen. Don't allow the day to dictate what you will or will not believe or attempt. You have the Word—the promise—and an oath by the Father. On top of all of this, He promised that He will never lie; for it is impossible for God to tell a lie. You have to believe that this is your day to start seeing God move greatly on your behalf, and it starts right now! Yes, God has promised to complete all that concerns you, and you can rest assured that none of His promises will fail.

Daily Prayer

Father God, thank you for watching over me and enabling me to complete all that you have placed in my power to do, in the Name of Jesus, Amen.

MY STRENGTH THROUGHOUT DAY

"For thou art my hope, O Lord God: thou art my trust from my youth."
Psalms 71:5 (KJV)

No matter what the day presents, keep your hope and faith intact. If you feel the spirit of depression, sadness, loneliness, or some hope-lessness, declare as the Psalmist did: "Why art thou cast down, O my soul? And why art thou disquieted in me? Know that God will not fail you, leave you, change on you, forsake you, nor break His promise to you. The Word declares: "They that trust in the Lord shall be as Mount Zion, which cannot be removed, but abideth forever." Keep in mind that "Happy is he that hath the Lord of Jacob for his help, whose hope is in the Lord his God." He is your strength and hope; trust Him today.

Daily Prayer

Father God, thank you for being my strength; my hope is in you for all my need, in the Name of Jesus, Amen.

THE UNCONDITIONAL LOVE OF THE FATHER

"You gave me life and showed me your unfailing love. My life was preserved by your care."

Job 10:12 (NLT)

Regardless of your past, your current situation, or what may transpire in the future, God's love for you is unconditional and unwavering. Moreover, as Apostle Paul declared: "For I am persuaded, that neither death, nor life, nor angels, nor principalities, nor powers, nor things present, nor things to come, nor height, nor depth, nor any other creature, shall be able to separate us from the love of God, which is in Christ Jesus our Lord." That's unwavering, unfailing love for us from the Father. John declared: "For God so loved the world that He gave His only begotten Son, that whosoever believeth in Him shall not perish but have everlasting life." Yes, regardless of what you do or don't do today, His love for you will not change.

Daily Prayer

Father God, thank you for your unfailing and unwavering love for me, a love that is unconditional and unending, in Jesus' Name, Amen.

THERE IS A TIME, PURPOSE, AND SEASON FOR IT ALL

"To every thing there is a season, and a time to every purpose under the heaven."

Ecclesiastes 3:1 (KJV)

God has a time and season for fulfilling every purpose in your life. Nothing is left to chance nor left to the will of any man. He is never late nor too early. He knows and controls the seasons in your life and can change them to fit the plan and purpose that He has for you each day. Never doubt His timing; it will always fit the purpose and time He has set for you. According to the Book of Daniel: "And He changes the times and the season: He removeth kings, and setteth up kings: He giveth wisdom unto the wise, and knowledge to them that know understanding." When it is your season, your time will come and do so without hesitation or delay. His time is perfect.

Daily Prayer

Father God, help me to be patient and wait for my time and season that I may fulfill the purpose that you have placed within me, in Jesus' Name, Amen.

HIGHER THOUGHTS AND WAYS THAN OURS

"For My thoughts are not your thoughts, neither are your ways my ways, saith the Lord."

Isaiah 55:8 (KJV)

God's thoughts of us are good and pleasant. In fact, Jeremiah declared: "I know the thoughts that I think toward you, saith the Lord, thoughts of peace, and not of evil, to give you an expected end." No matter what any man may think, say, or do; no one will or can change the thoughts that God thinks toward you. It matters not what others think. God's thoughts of you are only good, and they are meant to prosper you. The Psalmist declared: "Many, O Lord my God, are thy wonderful works which thou hast done, and thy thoughts which are to us-ward: they cannot be reckoned up in order unto thee: if I would declare and speak of them, they are more than can be numbered." God never thinks as we do, and His thoughts are unchanging towards us. Someone is thinking of you today, and they are good and pleasant ones.

Daily Prayer

Father God, thank you for always thinking of me and for always doing great things for me, in the Name of Jesus, Amen.

BORN TO OVERCOME

"For whatsoever is born of God overcometh the world..."

1 John 5:4 (KJV)

Whatever God gives birth to will overcome and thrive. Whatever God purposes shall come to pass. If it is of God, it will always overcome, and "if God be for you, who can be against you?" He is always mightier, stronger, wiser, bigger, and more powerful than anything that you will encounter on today. You are more than a conqueror through Christ Jesus our Lord. If God spoke it, it will come to pass just as He said, when He said it, and how He said it would happen. You do not have to worry or fear; if God be for you, nothing and no one can overcome you. Rest in knowing today that the Greater Than is on your side; none is greater.

Daily Prayer

Father God, thank you for empowering me in every area of my life, enabling me to overcome all my enemies, in the Name of Jesus, Amen.

THE AUTHOR AND FINISHER OF MY LIFE

"Looking unto Jesus the Author and Finisher of our faith..."
Hebrews 12:2 (KJV)

It is through Christ that we live, move, and have our existence. Everything begins with Him and ends with Him. He is the Author and Finisher of all that we do. The Gospel of John declares: "In the beginning was the Word, and the Word was with God, and the Word was God. The same was in the beginning with God. All things were made by Him, and without Him was not anything made that was made." God will perform all that is purposed for you on today. Expect it, embrace it, and decree it to be so. He truly is the Author and Finisher of your faith; trust Him for everything, not only today, but at all times. He will perfect all that concerns you without fail.

Daily Prayer

Father God, I look to you for all that I need on today, knowing that you will never forsake or leave me, in the Name of Jesus, Amen.

HE IS PAVING THE WAY BEFORE ME

"God is my strength and power: and He maketh my way perfect."
2 Samuel 22:33 (KJV)

We can do all things through Christ who strengthens us. He is our strength like no other, always going before us, leading us, caring for us, protecting us, and providing for us. He gives power to the weak and provides grace to us without merit. Apostle Paul declared: "And He said unto me, My grace is sufficient for thee: for my strength is made perfect in weakness." It is His strength that makes us strong and able to carry on, not ours. Moses declared: "The Lord is my strength and my song and He is become my salvation: He is my God, and I will prepare Him an habitation; my Father's God, and I will exalt Him." Rest in His strength today.

Daily Prayer

Father God, thank you for being my strength and all my help, in Jesus' Name, Amen.

HIS IS MY UNDERSTANDING

"O Lord, I know that the way of man is not in himself: it is not in man that walketh to direct his steps."

Jeremiah 10:23 (KJV)

Trust in the Lord with all of your heart; and lean not unto your own understanding. In all of your ways acknowledge Him, and He will direct your paths." Give your plans to Him and seek His directions. The promise is that your plans will be established. King Solomon declared: "We can make our own plans, but the Lord gives the right answers." Yes, commit everything that you plan to do to the Lord. Trust Him, and He will help you. It is His pleasure to make your way prosperous. Allowing the Holy Spirit to lead and guide you will assure you of this and other promises coming to pass. He will order your steps in and through His Word. Follow Him today.

Daily Prayer

Father God, please help me to walk according to your Word and the leading of the Holy Spirit, in the Name of Jesus, Amen.

LOOKING UNTO HIM FOR ALL OUR HELP

"Behold, the eye of the Lord is upon them that fear Him, upon them that hope in His mercy; to deliver their soul from death, and to keep them alive in famine."

Psalms 33:18-19 (KJV)

As believers, we are constantly lifting our eyes unto the hill from whence cometh our help, for our help comes from the Lord. The Lord is watching over us, keeping us, providing for us, and leading us throughout the day. Nothing good does he withhold from us because we are the righteousness of God through Christ Jesus. He feeds us, clothes us, shields us, and provides all that we need; for He is our Father. We are the apple of His eye, and nothing can change this or keep us from His amazing grace and mercy. When the enemy shall come in like a flood, the spirit of the Lord will lift up a standard against him, delivering us from all of the snares of the enemy. The Lord will prosper and bless you all day.

Daily Prayer

Father God, thank you for delivering me and for keeping me in your favor, in the Name of Jesus Amen.

UNCHANGEABLE PURPOSE

"For the Lord of hosts hath purposed, and who shall disannul it? And His hand is stretched out, and who shall turn it back?"

Isaiah 14:27 (KJV)

There is no plan "B" for your life. Why? Because God's plans never fail. God does not need to correct Himself or what He has prepared for you. Whatever God's purpose, no man is able to undo it. You are the apple of God's eye, and no one can pluck you out of His hands. All of His plans for you are going to be fulfilled in you on today. It is His pleasure to do so. He has not delivered you to leave you unto yourself. He will never forsake or leave you, "For it is God that worketh in you both to will and to do of His good pleasure." What God has for you far outweighs all that you will face on today, and nothing can undo this today or ever.

Daily Prayer

Father God, help me to walk in the purpose that you have for me on today that I might bring glory unto you, in the Name of Jesus, Amen.

IT WILL WORK ACCORDING TO HIS PLAN

"The Lord will work out His plans for my life—for your faithful love, O Lord, endures forever. Don't abandon me, for you made me."

Psalms 138:8 (NLT)

No matter what you have faced, are facing, or will face, the Lord will work out His plans for your life, not just today, but in the future as well. In any future situations or circumstances, you should testify that I know that God has seen me through them, and He will continue to see me through the unchartered path that I may embark upon each day. When experiencing setbacks and disappointments, you can remind the enemy that you are an overcomer, and God always causes you to triumph through Christ Jesus. Even if you have to wait on the Lord for longer than you anticipated, remind the enemy that God is never late nor has He ever missed an appointment. No, He will never abandon you but will always keep you in His care.

Daily Prayer

Father God, thank you for being my way when I cannot see a way, my provider when I am in need, and my joy, in Jesus' Name, Amen.

HE LIFTS ME DAILY

"From the end of the earth will I cry unto thee, when my heart is overwhelmed: lead me to the rock that is higher than I."

Psalms 61:2 (KJV)

God can and will lift up our bowed down heads, lifting us to higher heights in the spirit throughout the day. Decree today that in spite of what I've gone through, I know that I am BLESSED and KEPT by God. Ask the Father to help you on today to rest in His strength, stand upon His promises, follow His Holy Spirit, and declare the Word that you may fulfill all that God has already ordained for you to do. God may not answer the way you think He should; you should still give Him glory because you know that He loves you unconditionally. If your heart gets overwhelmed on today, know that God will lead you to the Rock that is higher than you are. If it seems on today that you can't figure things out, lift your eyes to the hills from whence cometh your help; your help cometh from the Lord.

Daily Prayer

Father God, thank you for leading me, lifting me, and comforting me throughout the day, in the Name of Jesus, Amen.

DRAWING NEAR UNTO THE FATHER

"But it is good for me to draw near to God: I have put my trust in the Lord God, that I may declare all thy works."

Psalms 73:28 (KJV)

The Book of James declared: "Draw nigh to God, and He will draw nigh to you. Cleanse your hands, ye sinners; and purify your hearts, ye double minded." Getting in the presence of the Lord will bring joy and life evermore; nothing can compare to being near to the Father. Jesus clearly explained the importance of being in His presence in the Gospel of Luke when He spoke to Martha about her concern that Mary was sitting at His feet listening to His teaching while she was doing chores around the house. Jesus said: "Martha, Martha, thou art careful and troubled about many things: But one thing is needful: and Mary hath chosen that good part, which shall not be taken away from her." In His presence is the fullness of Joy and life evermore. Enjoy this blessing today.

Daily Prayer

Father God, help me to remain in your presence, never trying to do anything without your guidance, in the Name of Jesus, Amen.

GREATENESS OF OUR GOD

"I know the greatness of the Lord – that our Lord is greater than any other god."

Psalms 135:5 (NLT)

The Psalmist reminds us: "Great is the Lord, and greatly to be praised; and His greatness is unsearchable." He is Lord of lords, King of kings, Alpha and Omega, the Beginning and the End, the Almighty God. There is absolutely nothing too difficult for God, and He is able to do exceeding abundantly above all that you can ask or think according to the power that works in you. The Prophet Isaiah declared: "To whom then will ye liken God? Or what likeness will ye compare unto Him?" This is who is fighting on your behalf and protecting you; if He is for you, and He certainly is, who can be against you on today? Don't worry. God is greater than anything that you will encounter on today.

Daily Prayer

Father God, I bless you and praise you for your greatness and love shown towards me every day, in the Name of Jesus, Amen.

FEAR THOU NOT, THE LORD

"For the Lord your God is He that goeth with you, to fight for you against your enemies, to save you."

Deuteronomy 20:4 (KJV)

There is no need to fear today. God is for you, and since He is, who can really be against you? There will be no enemy too big, no battle too difficult, nor any force that will be greater than the Lord God. You can rest assured that "No weapon that is formed against thee shall prosper; and every tongue that shall rise against thee in judgment thou shalt condemn. This is the heritage of the servants of the Lord, and their righteousness is of me, saith the Lord." After the Lord delivered the children of Israel from the Egyptian army, the people declared: "The Lord is my strength and song, and He is become my salvation: He is my God, and I will prepare Him an habitation; my father's God, and I will exalt Him. The Lord is a man of war: the Lord is His Name."

Daily Prayer

Father God, thank you for always fighting for me and leading me to victory over my enemies, in the Name of Jesus, Amen.

FAITHFUL IS OUR GOD

"Know therefore that the Lord thy God, He is God, the faithful God, which keepeth covenant and mercy with them that love Him and keep His commandments to a thousand generations."

Deuteronomy 7:9 (KJV)

You can rest assured that God will always keep His promises, regardless of the situation or circumstance. He is not a man that He should lie; He is faithful to His Word. Even when we are faithless, He is faithful. Your day may be filled with challenges, opportunities, and some uncertainties; however, through them all, you can count on the faithfulness of the Lord God. He will remain faithful to you throughout the day. So, regardless of what you face on today, because you are the righteousness of God through Christ Jesus, nothing good will be withheld from you—regardless! Declare today as Apostle Paul did: "And the Lord shall deliver me from every evil work, and will preserve me unto His heavenly Kingdom." Take Him at His Word.

Daily Prayer

Father God, thank you for always keeping your word and promises made unto me; not for me only but for my seed after me, in the Name of Jesus, Amen.

HE BRINGS US OUT FOR HIS GLORY

"And He brought us out from thence, that He might bring us in, to give us the land which He sware unto our fathers."

Deuteronomy 6:23 (KJV)

Today, you can rest assured that God is able to deliver you, regardless of the battle, the struggle, or the situation. Nothing is too difficult for Him to do for you. You can declare with confidence as the Psalmist did: "The Lord is my Rock, and my fortress, and my deliverer; my God, my strength, in whom I will trust; my buckler, and the horn of my salvation, and my high tower." He also declared: "Unto thee, O my strength, will I sing: for God is my defense, and the God of my mercy." We can "call upon Him, and He will hear us: He will be with us in trouble; He will deliver us, and honor us." He can and will bring us out all right.

Daily Prayer

Father God, thank you for being faithful to your Word and for always delivering me from the hands of my enemies, in the Name of Jesus, Amen.

HE ORDERS MY STEPS

"The steps of a good man are ordered by the Lord: and he delighteth in His way."

Psalms 37:23 (KJV)

King Solomon declared: "A man's heart deviseth his way: but the Lord directeth his steps." Don't be rushed into making a decision or plan to do anything without praying for directions, seeking godly counsel, and taking your time to decide. "Trust in the Lord with all thine heart; and lean not unto thine own understanding. In all thy ways, acknowledge Him, and He shall direct thy paths." Yes, wait upon the Lord and watch Him direct thy way. God through His Word is "a lamp unto our feet, and a light unto our paths." We can safely trust in Him, knowing that He always fulfills His promises, all of them. Allow Him to direct your steps today. He's ready.

Daily Prayer

Father God, please direct me in the paths that you would have me to travel on today, in the Name of Jesus, Amen.

WE WILL OVERCOME OUR ENEMIES

"The God of my mercy shall prevent me: God shall let me see my desire upon my enemies."

Psalms 59:10 (KJV)

"When the enemy shall come in like a flood, the Spirit of the Lord will lift up a standard against him." This is a promise of deliverance from the Lord, and there is nothing that the enemy can do about it. You will have opposition, but God has promised you that no weapon that is formed against you will prosper. The trials will come, but know that God is always faithful, and He will never allow anything to fall upon you that you cannot bear. People may change, but remember that God will not; for He is the same yesterday, today, and forever. You will not be at the mercy of any man today or ever. You can know that God has given you favor because your enemy has not triumphed over you. You will see the victory.

Daily Prayer

Father God, thank you for giving me the neck of my enemies and for the victory that I enjoy daily, in Jesus' Name, Amen.

NEW MERCIES EACH DAY

"Great is His faithfulness; His mercies begin afresh each morning."
Lamentations 3:23 (NLT)

Don't worry, and try not to give any thoughts to giving up; for the promises of God are greater than the issues and struggles that my confront you! No matter your issues from yesterday, regardless of yesterday's setbacks, God has given you brand new mercies on today. As sure as night follows day, you will be granted this new mercy at the beginning of each day. You can go throughout the day knowing that not only does God care about you deeply, but He also loves you unconditionally. Today, regardless of the challenges, regardless of the trials, the faithfulness of God should keep you encouraged no matter what confronts you, knowing that God is there for you.

Daily Prayer

Father God, thank you for granting me new mercies today, mercies that I don't deserve but am so appreciative of, in Jesus' Name, Amen.

TOMORROW WILL TAKE CARE OF ITSELF

"So don't worry about tomorrow, for tomorrow will bring its own worries..."
Matthew 6:34 (NLT)

God has not given us the spirit of fear, but of power, and of love, and of a sound mind. Worrying about what may or may not happen is not productive and can distract you from the blessings of today. What has or has not happened is past; what is before you today is what should have your attention. Yesterday is past. You are responsible for now, and the future is God's responsibility. Be anxious for nothing, but in prayer with supplications make your request known unto the Lord. You do your best to take full advantage of today, and let the Lord take care of what may or may not happen tomorrow. He specializes in this.

Daily Prayer

Father God, help me to cast all my cares upon you and not worry about what may or may not take place tomorrow, in the Name of Jesus, Amen.

LET'S DECLARE HIS MIGHTY WORKS

"The Lord hath brought forth our righteousness: come, and let us declare in Zion the work of the Lord our God."

Jeremiah 51:10 (KJV)

The prophet spoke in 1 Chronicles: "Give thanks unto the Lord, call upon His name, make known his deeds among the people. Let's tell of the goodness of the Lord, that others may glorify the His Name." The Psalmist declared: "I will sing of the mercies of the Lord forever: with my mouth will I make known thy faithfulness to all generations." Tell of His goodness, share with others the wonderful power, the unconditional love, and his grace and mercy with those whom He places in your path today. Know for a certainty that if He is lifted up, He will draw all men unto Himself. Praise the Lord from whom all blessings flow.

Daily Prayer

Father God, it is an honor and privilege to testify of your mighty works and tell of your goodness; help me to never be ashamed to lift you up, in the Name of Jesus, Amen.

GOD WILL NOT FORGET YOUR LABOR

"For God is not unrighteous to forget your work and labor of love, which ye have shewed toward His Name, in that ye have ministered to the saints, and do minister."

Hebrews 6:10 (KJV)

Your work, your labor, your service will not go unrewarded. God will not forget what you have done in and for the Kingdom. "Be not weary in well doing, for in due season you will reap, if you faint not." The Prophet Isaiah declared: "Can a woman forget her sucking child, that she should not have compassion on the son of her womb? Yea, they may forget, yet will I not forget thee." It is impossible for God to be late, unfair, or forgetful. Nor will He overlook you. You may have waited while others seem to have gotten ahead of you; however, the timing of God is also perfect. Be not discouraged; you are not forgotten nor will you be. Trust Him now.

Daily Prayer

Father God, thank you for never forgetting about me but always coming to my rescue, regardless of my position or condition, in Jesus' Name, Amen.

GOD DOES ANSWER US

*"He shall call upon me, and I will answer him: I will be with him in trou-
ble; I will deliver him, and honor him."*

Psalms 91:15 (KJV)

No matter what it looks like at the moment, know for a certainty that God is not asleep at the wheel. Jeremiah encouraged us to
"Call unto the Lord, and He will answer us, and shew us great and
mighty things, which we do not know." We are not waiting on Him,
but He is waiting on us. Remember, death and life are in the power of the tongue, and we have the authority to decree something
and it shall be established unto us. Moreover, if we have the faith,
we can speak those things that be not as though they were already
done. Ask, and it shall be given; seek, and ye shall find it; knock, and
it will be opened unto you. Don't be afraid to call on Him today.

Daily Prayer

Father God, thank you for answering me when I call and never turning a
dull ear unto my cry, in Jesus' Name, Amen.

THE LORD IS OUR EXPECTATION

"My soul, wait thou only upon God; for my expectation is from Him."
Psalms 62:5 (KJV)

Your expectations build your Hope; your hope builds your Faith. Expect it, hope for it, have faith that it will be done! Others' disbelief does not make the promise of God to you untrue! It's your faith, your hope, your expectation – not theirs – that matters. Don't become discouraged because of doubt and disbelief of others; God knows what you have been promised. Expect God to show Himself mighty on your behalf today, knowing that nothing is impossible to them that believe. Walk by faith and not by sight, and watch God make all things available to you. God is your expectation, and His resources are unlimited.

Daily Prayer

Father God, you are my hope and my expectation; all my help comes from you, in Jesus' Name, Amen.

VICTORY IN CHRIST JESUS

"But thanks be to God, which giveth us the victory through our Lord Jesus Christ."

1 Corinthians 15:57 (KJV)

Because of the finished work of Christ at Calvary, we have the victory over the enemy. King David declared: "Thou art my hiding place; thou shalt preserve me from trouble; thou shalt compass me about with songs of deliverance." This is a great promise to remind your enemy of today. If it's of God, you can count on provisions, protection, direction, assistance, favor, and covering. Yes, you will have opposition; however, it will not be able to overcome what God can produce on your behalf. You will have a testimony, one that will remind others of God's amazing favor on your life. Rejoice, God has already given you what is needed for your victory.

Daily Prayer

Father God, thank you for empowering me throughout the day, giving me the victory over all my enemies, in the Name of Jesus, Amen.

WE OVERCOME THROUGH CHRIST

"For whatsoever is born of God overcometh the world..."

1 John 5:4 (KJV)

There will always be a battle, a fight, a struggle, and some sacrifices that are necessary to change a situation. Know that if you are engaged in a struggle or fight, you are probably making a change in some situation; keep up the fight. "When the enemy shall come in like a flood, the Spirit will lift up a standard against him." Whatever God gives life to will win, regardless of the position, circumstance, or situation. Nothing can be taken from you that God has determined is necessary for your success. Be faithful, be consistent, and be committed; and you will see God do awesome things for you throughout the day. He will cause you to overcome and fulfill what He has purposed for you today.

Daily Prayer

Father God, thank you for birthing in me your will for today; please help me to stay focused so that I do not become distracted for this purpose, in Jesus' Name, Amen.

GUIDING MY PATH DAILY

"He restoreth my soul: He leadeth me in the paths of righteousness for His Name's sake."

Psalms 23:3 (KJV)

"The steps of a good man are ordered by the Lord: and He delighteth in His way." Since this is so, then wherever we find ourselves, it may be by His orders. He does it, of course, through His Word. Yes, His Word is a lamp unto our feet and a light unto our path. He will lead us unto our wealthy place based upon His unconditional love for us. David was so confident in the leading of the Lord that He further declared: "Yea, though I walk through the valley of the shadow of death, I will fear no evil: for thou art with me; thy rod and thy staff they comfort me." Be encouraged today, for "He will not suffer your foot to be moved: He that keepeth thee will not slumber."

Daily Prayer

Father God, thank you for leading me in the path that you have ordained for me today, in the Name of Jesus, Amen.

WORDS THAT SATISFY BY MY WORDS

"A man's belly shall be satisfied with the fruit of his mouth; and with the increase of is lips shall he be filled."

Proverbs 18:20 (KJV)

It is by your words that your heart will be filled and you become satisfied. Remember, death and life are in the power of the tongue. Use your words to speak life to what has become dormant and to speak destruction to that which would bring harm to you or your surroundings. Speak God's Word over every situation, over every condition, to every circumstance, and believe it to be done in the Name of Jesus. Job declared: "Thou shalt decree a thing and it shall be established unto you." Yes, your belly (soul) shall be satisfied with the words that come out of your mouth, and you will continue to be filled with what you continually say. Speak life to it today.

Daily Prayer

Father God, please help me to control what I say so that I will only speak words that build up those around me, in the Name of Jesus, Amen.

HE DOES WONDERS FOR US

"Who is like unto thee, O Lord, among the gods? Who is like thee, glorious in holiness, fearful in praises, doing wonders?"

Exodus 15:11 (KJV)

Our expectations are in the Lord God through Christ Jesus. No matter what man or the world's system offers, our expectations are rooted and grounded in Christ. There is none like unto Him, and nothing is too difficult for Him to fulfill for you on today. God has not changed; His Word has not changed; His Grace has not diminished nor His mercy decreased. God is able today to do more than you can ask think or do according to the power that worketh in us. The Lord will save, heal, cover, provide, and lead you throughout the day, knowing that we cannot do anything without Him. Capture the momen; it has been given to you for a reason.

Daily Prayer

Father God, thank you for enabling me to succeed today in the things that you have planned for me, in the Name of Jesus, Amen.

THE POWER OF HIS WORD

"All scripture is given by inspiration of God, and is profitable for doctrine, for reproof, for correction, for instruction in righteousness."

2 Timothy 3:16 (KJV)

The Word of the Lord is still true; stand on it regardless of the situation or circumstance. You can stand on the Word, for God will not lie. You can declare as the Psalmist did: "As for God, His way is perfect; the Word of the Lord is tried: He is a buckler to all them that trust in Him." The Hebrew writer declared: "For the Word of God is quick, and powerful, and sharper than any two-edged sword, piercing even to the dividing asunder of soul and spirit, and of the joints and marrow, and is a discerner of the thoughts and intents of the heart." Therefore, whatever you need for directions, corrections, or encouragement, you can find it all in the Word of God.

Daily Prayer

Father God, help me to walk according to your Word that I might not sin against you, in Jesus' Name, Amen.

FAITHFULNESS PRODUCES BLESSINGS

"Moreover it is required in stewards, that a man be found faithful."
1 Corinthians 4:2 (KJV)

To the best of your ability, stay faithful regardless of the opposition or situation. Scripture reminds us that the faithful shall abound in blessings. Luke declared: "And He said unto him, Well done, thou good and faithful servant: because thou hast been faithful in a very little, have thou authority over ten cities." Faithfulness will cause promotion! Stay focused, stay committed, and stay encouraged, for the Lord God is with you for the duration of the fight. Regardless of the traps, roadblocks, schemes, plans, or efforts of your enemies, decree as King David did: "The Lord is on my side, I will not fear: what can man do unto me?" We are told to be "thou faithful until death, and He will give us a crown of life."

Daily Prayer

Father God, help me to remain faithful in all that I have been given to do, never being slothful in my duties, in the Name of Jesus, Amen.

SAFE IN HIS ARMS

"For in the time of trouble He shall hide me in His pavilion: in the secret of His tabernacle shall He hide me; He shall set me up upon a rock."

Psalms 27:5 (KJV)

God knows how to keep us from falling and to present us faultless before the presence of His Glory. We are never left unprotected, never without angelic presence; for "There shall no evil befall thee, neither shall any plague come nigh thy dwelling. For He shall give His angels charge over thee, to keep thee in all thy ways. They shall bear thee up in their hands, lest thou dash thy foot against a stone." He will always be a present help in the time of trouble. The Lord will be your protector throughout the day, and nothing is too difficult for Him to do for you. Regardless of the surroundings, the Word of the Lord assures us that "if God be for us, who can be against us?" Fear thou not, for He will hide you in the safety of His arms throughout the day.

Daily Prayer

Father God, thank you for keeping me protected throughout the day, shielding me, and keeping me safe in your arms, in Jesus' Name, Amen.

GRACE AND MERCY ENDURETH FOREVER

"Thou art my God, and I will praise thee: thou art my God, I will exalt thee.
O give thanks unto the Lord; for He is good: for His mercy endureth forever."
Psalms 118: 28-29 (KJV)

Nothing you will face today or in the future can outlast, outdo, outperform, or overpower the grace and mercy of the Lord God Almighty. The Lord is good, His mercy is everlasting, and His truth endureth unto all generations. David said: "Surely goodness and mercy shall follow me all the days of my life, and I will dwell in the house of the Lord forever." His grace shall empower you, and His mercy will comfort you throughout any ordeal or situation that you may encounter during the day. Don't worry or fear: God knows what you have need of before you even ask Him. You can rest assured that this Grace and mercy will far outlast anything that you will have to face today. Rejoice today: God has you in His arms.

Daily Prayer

Father God, thank you for your endless grace and your everlasting mercy, in the Name of Jesus, Amen.

MORE FOR US THAN AGAINST US

"There shall not any man be able to stand before thee all the days of thy life: as I was with Moses, so I will be with thee: I will not fail thee, nor forsake thee."

Joshua 1:5 (KJV)

Always, always keep in mind that there are more for you than are against you. Greater is He that is in you than he that is in the world. Since God is always for us, the odds are always in our favor. The Psalmist declared: "The Lord is my light and my salvation; whom shall I fear? The Lord is the strength of my life; of whom shall I be afraid? When the wicked, even my foes, came upon me to eat up my flesh, they stumbled and fell." You can rest with confidence that in the time of trials or trouble, the Lord will be that present help. You can rejoice today; help is already there for you. He will not forsake or leave you.

Daily Prayer

Father God, thank you for being my secure place and my strong tower that I can run to regardless of my situation, in the Name of Jesus, Amen.

MOVING FORWARD WITH CONFIDENCE

"The Lord our God spake unto us in Horeb, saying, Ye have dwelt long enough in this mount: Turn you, and take your journey..."

Deuteronomy 1:6-7 (KJV)

Today is too important and too critical for us to focus on what did or did not happen on yesterday or in our past. We have far too great a blessing coming to allow the failures of yesterday to consume us! We cannot afford to continue to circle the same mountain (decision, plan, or place) that confronts us without moving over or around it. The Lord is with us, and He will enable us to move successfully over or through our mountains, roadblocks, or distractions. We can't afford to allow what did not happen to keep us looking back and wondering instead of looking forward to all that God has prepared for us on today. God is able to perfect all that concerns us, and He is never late with His promises.

Daily Prayer

Father God, I pray today that you will help me to move forward in the things that you have given for me to complete, regardless of the obstacles that may try to block my path, in Jesus' Name, Amen.

WHO OR WHAT CAN OVERCOME

"Then will the Lord drive out all these nations from before you, and ye shall possess greater nations and mightier than yourselves."
Deuteronomy 11:23 (KJV)

The Lord will go before us throughout the day, always providing for us, leading us, and caring for us for our profit. God is for us, so who really can successfully fight against us? If we were not being successful or doing something right, do you think we would be receiving the attacks, the smears, closed doors, rejections, or battles from the enemy? Of course not. However, we cannot afford to allow any of the aforementioned events to prevent us from pursuing our God-ordained mission. No matter who has walked away; no matter how big the enemy may be, God is greater and will see us through to victory. It is God who will cause us to possess the new land.

Daily Prayer

Father God, thank you for allowing me to conquer that which attacks me on a daily basis, always looking unto you, the Author and finisher of my faith, in Jesus' Name, Amen.

EMPOWERED BY THE LORD GOD

*"And with great power gave the apostles witness of the resurrection of the
Lord Jesus: and great grace was upon them all."*

Acts 4:33 (KJV)

All power belongs unto the Lord God, and He will empower us to victory on today. The Psalmist declared: "No good thing will He withhold from them that walk uprightly." The Book of Acts declared: "But ye shall receive power, after that the Holy Ghost is come upon you: and ye shall be witnesses unto me both in Jerusalem, and in all Judaea, and in Samaria, and unto the uttermost part of the earth." Remember, Apostle Paul reminded us that "We can do all things through Christ Jesus who strengthens (enables) us." Yes, all power belongs to God, and He chooses who will be blessed with this power from on high. Trust Him today to empower you to be victorious over all that confronts you.

Daily Prayer

Father God, thank you for empowering me today to fulfill all that you have given me to do and not allowing the enemy to triumph over me, in the Name of Jesus, Amen.

LET'S TRY IT IN JESUS' NAME

"Give a portion to seven, and also to eight; for thou knowest not what evil shall be upon the earth."

Ecclesiastes 11:2 (KJV)

God is a God who changes not, but He does do new things. Regardless of what did or did not happen yesterday, He has given us new mercies on today. However, nothing will be different from yesterday or the days before if we keep doing the same things. We will keep getting the same treatment as before if we keep associating/engaging with the same kind of people or situations. If we leave our results in the hands of others, we will get their results and not ours. Look for God to do new things, and be willing to follow the leading of the Holy Spirit to be successful in them. Make this day yours, and don't allow the failures or missteps of yesterday to keep you from pursuing new endeavors.

Daily Prayer

Father God, thank you for doing new things to and for me, allowing me to pursue the new endeavors that you have allowed to come my way, in Jesus' Name, Amen.

LOVE LIKE CHRIST

"He that loveth not knoweth not God; for God is love."

1 John 4:8 (KJV)

Jesus declared that "By this shall all men know that ye are my disciples, if ye have love one to another." Apostle Paul declared: "And now abideth faith, hope, and charity, these three; but the greatest of these is charity." We are to love just as Christ loved us and gave Himself for us. The Apostle John declared: "Beloved, let us love one another: for love is of God; and everyone that loveth is born of God, and knoweth God. He that loveth not knoweth not God, for God is love. In this was manifested the love of God toward us, because that God sent His only begotten Son into the world, that we might live through Him." Again, "He that loveth not, knoweth not God for God is love." This has to be our mindset for all that we do and say concerning others.

Daily Prayer

Father God, thank you for loving me; please help me to love others in like manner, in the Name of Jesus, Amen.

THE LORD WILL LIFT US UP AGAIN

"For a just man falleth seven times, and riseth up again: but the wicked shall fall into mischief."

Proverbs 24:16 (KJV)

The Apostle John declared: "If we confess our sins, He is faithful and just to forgive us our sins, and to cleanse us from all unrighteousness." The Psalmist declared: "The steps of a good man are ordered by the Lord: and he delighteth in his way. Though he fall, he shall not be utterly cast down: for the Lord upholdeth him with His hand. I have been young, and now am old; yet have I not seen the righteous forsaken, nor his seed begging bread. He is ever merciful, and lendeth; and his seed is blessed." He is a God of another chance, as many as He sees necessary. No matter what, God is not going to abandon you. Rest confidently in this promise today.

Daily Prayer

Father God, thank you for always restoring me, lifting me, and placing me back on the right path, in the Name of Jesus, Amen.

WE CAN DO NOTHING WITHOUT HIM

"I am the Vine, ye are the branches: He that abideth in me, and I in him, the same bringeth forth much fruit: for without me ye can do nothing."

John 15:5 (KJV)

"I am the Vine, ye are the branches: He that abideth in me, and I in him, the same bringeth forth much fruit: for without me ye can do nothing." Without Christ, we are helpless and can do absolutely nothing. Without Christ, life is meaningless, hopeless, and certainly will not end well. As we may recall, "We can do all things through Christ who strengthens us," and nothing is impossible for God to do on our behalf. However, without Him, we can do nothing. John clearly reminds us that we must "Abide in Him, and He in us. As the branch cannot bear fruit of itself, except it abide in the vine; no more can ye, except ye abide in me. I am the Vine, ye are the branches: He that abideth in Me, and I in him, the same bringeth forth much fruit: FOR WITHOUT ME YE CAN DO NOTHING." Don't try it without Him.

Daily Prayer

Father God, I thank you for allowing me to complete what you have given me to do through Christ Jesus, Amen.

THE CLOSER WE GET TO HIM, THE CLOSER HE WILL BE TO US

"Draw nigh to God, and He will draw nigh to you. Cleanse your hands, ye sinners; and purify your hearts, ye double minded."

James 4:8 (KJV)

James allows us to see that when we make it our effort to draw close to the Father, He will in turn draw close to us. The Gospel according to Matthew encouraged us to "Come unto me, all ye that labour and are heavy laden, and I will give you rest. Take my yoke upon you, and learn of me; for I am meek and lowly in heart: and ye shall find rest unto your souls. For my yoke is easy, and my burden is light." God is not far from us; in fact, He is a present help at all times for us. Isaiah declared: "Behold, the Lord's hand is not shortened, that it cannot save; neither his ear heavy, that it cannot hear: But your iniquities have separated between you and your God, and your sins have hid His face from you, that He will not hear." He wants to be close to you today.

Daily Prayer

Father God, help me to walk in closeness with you so that I may never attempt anything without your guidance, in the Name of Jesus, Amen.

A GLAD HEART IS GOOD MEDICINE

"A cheerful heart is good medicine, but a broken spirit saps a person's strength."

Proverbs 17:22 (NLT)

Do all that you can to be sure that nothing steals your joy today. The enemy knows that the joy of the Lord is your strength, and if he can get you to walk in sadness and sorrow, then you will not be walking in the strength of the Holy Spirit. Be as happy as possible; it's a gift from the Father. Sadness is not God-given and is a spirit to steal your joy, thereby making you weak. Yes, a merry heart doeth good like a medicine; be sure to take a daily dose each morning. The Psalmist declared: "Lift up your heads, O ye gates: and be ye lifted up, ye everlasting doors; and the King of Glory shall come in. Who is the King of Glory: The Lord strong and mighty, the Lord mighty in battle." Remember: "Rejoice, and again I say, rejoice."

Daily Prayer

Father God, help me to walk in the Joy of knowing you so that my heart stays cheerful at all times, in the Name of Jesus, Amen.

ABUNDANT LIFE IN CHRIST

"The thief cometh not, but for to steal, and to kill, and to destroy: I am come that they might have life, and that they might have it more abundantly."

John 10:10 (KJV)

Whatever takes you away from your God-ordained purpose or call is of the enemy. Remember, he only comes but for to steal, kill, or destroy what God has givens you or called you to do. Today, be diligent to watch what confronts you, bearing in mind that God will not send anything or anyone that would cause you to be pulled away from the things He as placed in your life. Third John reminds us that the Father "wish[es] above all things that thou mayest prosper and be in health, even as thy soul prospereth." Remember, "Every good and every perfect gift is from above, and cometh down from the Father of lights with whom is no variableness, neither shadow of turning." If it's good, it's good. Period.

Daily Prayer

Father God, thank you for always blessing me with good things; please help me to know when it is the enemy that attempts to bring things into my life, in the Name of Jesus, Amen.

CONSIDER IT ALREADY DONE

"And it shall come to pass, that before they call, I will answer; and while they are yet speaking, I will hear."

Isaiah 65:24 (KJV)

We are told to be anxious about nothing, but through prayer with supplications, let our request be made known unto the Lord. The Father knows what we have need of before we even ask Him. He said in Matthew: "... What man is there of you, whom if his son ask bread, will he give him a stone? Or if he ask a fish, we he give him a serpent? If ye then, being evil, know how to give good gifts unto your children, how much more shall your Father which is in heaven give good things to them that ask him? Ask, and it will be given; seek, and ye shall find it; knock, it will be opened unto you." Look today for unexpected, unexplained blessings to come to you.

Daily Prayer

Father God, I will continue to lift my eyes unto the hills from whence my help comes; all my help comes from you, in the Name of Jesus, Amen.

IT'S ALL IN HIS HANDS

"The king's heart is in the hand of the Lord, as the rivers of water: He turneth it whithersoever He will."

Proverbs 21:1 (KJV)

From this word for Solomon, it is clear that every leader's heart is in the hands of the Lord. Regardless if he or she is good or evil. It is God who removes kings and sets up kings. Keep in mind that God has the power to move the king's heart in any direction that He wills. Our prayers should be that God would prick the hearts of those in authority that they would govern in a godly manner. It is through Christ that we live, move, and have our being; and without Him, nothing is possible. If there someone that seems to be ungodly, treating you in hostile manner, you have the power to pray to the Father to have that person's heart be changed as God sees fit. Trust Him today.

Daily Prayer

Father God, the king's heart is in your hands. I pray today that you will turn the hearts of leaders everywhere in the direction that you would have them to lead, in Jesus' Name, Amen.

GODLY PEACE THROUGH CHRIST

"And the peace of God, which passeth all understanding, shall keep your hearts and minds through Christ Jesus."

Philippians 4:7 (KJV)

God does not give us peace based upon things, people, situations, or circumstances but based upon His promises and presence in our lives. Worry is not God-sent; therefore, it's an enemy of ours and should not be allowed to have access to our lives. It is a thief of our peace, our contentment, our happiness, and of our faith. "Don't worry about anything; instead pray about everything. Tell God what you need, and thank Him for all He has done" (Philippians 4:6 NLT). It is the assurance that God is constant, faithful, and good that keeps us safe and secure. It is His peace, not ours, that guards our hearts and minds all through Christ Jesus. Trust Him for peace in all things today.

Daily Prayer

Father God, thank you for your peace that keeps my mind and heart safely trusting in you, in Jesus' Name, Amen.

OPEN DOORS FROM THE FATHER

"For a great door and effectual is opened unto me, and there are many adversaries."

1 Corinthians 16:9 (KJV)

Every door that is opened unto you is because of the the Lord God. It is He who opens doors of opportunities, blessings, and favor to you. Job declared: "Behold, He breaketh down, and it cannot be built again: He shutteth up a man, and there can be no opening." Every blessing comes from above, and with it will come adversaries. However, the same God that opened the door for you is the same God who can keep it opened. Ask, and you will receive; seek, and you will find it; knock, and it will be opened unto you. There is an open door that only God can open for you. Declare today as the Prophet Isaiah did: "Arise, shine; for thy light is come, and the glory of the Lord is risen upon thee." It's your open door.

Daily Prayer

Father God, thank you for my open doors, doors that only you can open. Please help me to discern the ones that are not from you, in Jesus' Name, Amen.

THE HOLY SPIRIT HAS GIVEN US LIBERTY

"Now the Lord is that Spirit: and where the Spirit of the Lord is, there is liberty."

2 Corinthians 3:17 (KJV)

Where the Spirit of the Lord is there is liberty, liberty that only Christ can bring. It's never the position, situation, circumstance, or place, for Christ is the Spirit; and wherever the Spirit is there is liberty. Greet each day with expectations; meet each challenge with the confidence of knowing that God is for you; face the enemy knowing that the presence of the Lord is going before you; declare that "no weapon that is formed against me shall prosper." You are not in bondage to anyone or anything, and because of the blood of Christ and His finished work at Calvary, your liberty is guaranteed for life. Expect God's best today, for you can never exhaust His grace and mercy. They are free through Christ Jesus.

Daily Prayer

Father God, thank you for freeing me from all that would have me in bondage, in the Name of Jesus, Amen.

SEEING BEYOND THE NATURAL

"But as it is written, Eye hath not seen, nor ear heard, neither have entered into the heart of man, the things which God hath prepared for them that love him."

1 Corinthians 2:9 (KJV)

The natural man cannot see what God has prepared for those who love Him. It may seem too farfetched, too unreal, or impossible to achieve. However, God, through His Holy Spirit, has or will reveal them to us. We walk by faith and not by what we see in the natural. The enemy has no clue what God is going to do for you on today; therefore, you can rejoice in knowing that God is watching over you to fulfill all that He would have you to do on today. According to Apostle Paul: "God hath revealed them unto us by His Spirit: for the Spirit searcheth all things, yea, the deep things of God." If we are led by the Spirit, we will see the things that God has prepared for us. Let Him lead you on today.

Daily Prayer

Father God, thank you for leading me today so that I will see those things that you have prepared for me, in the Name of Jesus, Amen.

ACCORDING TO HIS PURPOSE

"In whom also we have obtained an inheritance, being predestinated according to the purpose of Him who worketh all things after the counsel of His own will."

Ephesians 1:11 (KJV)

According to 1 Chronicles: "Both riches and honor come of God, and He reighnest over all; and in His hand is power and might; and in His hand it is to make great, and to give strength unto all." It is God who determines when, where, and how your promotion will occur. Remember, "Every good gift, and every perfect gift is from above, and cometh down from the Father of lights, with whom is no variableness, neither shadow of turning." Everything that God does in your life is based upon His will, not yours. Apostle Paul made this clear when he stated: "It is God that worketh in you both to will, and to do of His good pleasure." It's His will that will be done in your life today; allow Him to lead you to His desired place on today.

Daily Prayer

Father God, thank you for working in me to will and to do your will, in the Name of Jesus, Amen.

THE ABILITY TO UNDERSTAND

"Wisdom is the principal thing; therefore, get wisdom: and with all thy getting get understanding."

Proverbs 4:7 (KJV)

Each day, pray for the understanding to apply the wisdom that you have to move throughout the day. Wisdom without understanding will lead to frustration and mistakes. King Solomon declared that "Wisdom is better than strength" and that "Wisdom is a defence, and money is a defence: but the excellency of knowledge is, that wisdom giveth life to them that have it." Moreover, the Word declares: "Happy is the man that findeth wisdom, and the man that getteth understanding. For the merchandise of it is better than the merchandise of silver, and the gain thereof than fine gold. She is more precious than rubies: and all the things thou canst desire are not compared unto her." With all of thy getting, get understanding.

Daily Prayer

Father God, help me to walk in understanding so that I can apply the wisdom that you have given me, in the Name of Jesus, Amen.

HE ALWAYS KEEPS HIS PROMISE

"The Lord is not slack concerning His promise, as some men count slackness; but is longsuffering to us-ward, not willing that any should perish, but that all should come to repentance."

2 Peter 3:9 (KJV)

You can rest assured, God will always keep His promise to you. God has not forgotten what is promised to you nor has He changed His mind about things concerning you! God will never be late, never miss an assignment, nor forget His promise to you. Regardless of your current situation or condition, God's promise is still the same concerning you. Whatever you are facing today, know for a certainty that there is a promise from God concerning it. You can search the scriptures and find the promise that God has for you and take Him at His Word. He is God, and He changes not, no matter what the current situation or condition looks like. He is and will not be slack concerning His promises to you on today. Trust Him with all that concerns you.

Daily Prayer

Father God, thank you for your promises to me and for always fulfilling every one of them in its season, in Jesus' Name, Amen.

SEEKING THE MIND OF CHRIST

"For who hath known the mind of the Lord, that he may instruct Him? But we have the mind of Christ."

1 Corinthians 2:16 (KJV)

"The Word states: "Thou wilt keep him in perfect peace, whose mind is stayed on thee." We are told to "let this mind be in us, which was also in Christ Jesus: Who, being in the form of God, thought it not robbery to be equal with God." Keeping a mind that is sensitive to the leading of the Holy Spirit, open to receiving what God has said, and willing to be led by the Holy Spirit is essential to living the life that God has ordained for a believer. Having the mind of Christ has great benefits. Apostle Paul declared: "Casting down imaginations, and every high thing that exalteth itself against the knowledge of God, and being every thought to the obedience of Christ."

Daily Prayer

Father God, please help me to keep my mind on you and the Kingdom as I walk through the day, in Name of Jesus, Amen.

GREATER IS COMING

"The glory of this latter house shall be greater than of the former, saith the Lord of hosts: and in this place will I give peace, saith the Lord of hosts."

Haggai 2:9 (KJV)

What's coming for you is greater than what has been. God will never do less for you than before. Always expect God to be more than enough, and He will always do more for you, regardless of what has been done for you in the past. Your current situation or position cannot compete with what God has planned and purposed for your life. Nothing can undo what He can cause to come to pass for you on today. People or things can come against you, fight against you, and even plot against you; but God's plans for you on today are in His hands, not theirs. Know that your current situation and circumstance are not your final position. Trust God.

Daily Prayer

Father God, thank you for always making things better for me than they have ever been, in the Name of Jesus, Amen.

HE WILL SUBDUE OUR ENEMIES

"For the Lord Most High is terrible; He is a great King over all the earth. He shall subdue the people under us, and the nations under our feet."
Psalms 47:2-3 (KJV)

God will give you the victory over your enemies, regardless of who they might be. The Psalmist gave us encouragement in reference to our help from the Lord when he stated: "The Lord is my light and my salvation; whom shall I fear? The Lord is the strength of my life; of whom shall I be afraid? When the wicked, even mine enemies and my foes, came upon me to eat up my flesh, they stumbled and fell. Though an host should encamp against me, my heart shall not fear: though war should rise against me, in this will I be confident." Through Christ, you can be more than a conqueror. You can be certain that the King of kings and the Lord of lords is on your side today, and "no weapon that is formed against you shall prosper."

Daily Prayer

Father God, thank you for being on my side and for making me victorious over the attacks of my enemies, in the Name of Jesus, Amen.

RESTING IN CHRIST JESUS

"Come unto Me, all ye that labour and are heavy laden, and I will give you rest."

Matthew 11:28 (KJV)

It is through Christ that we live, move, and have our being; and there is really no peace or joy without Him. There are things that we try to do on our own that will never succeed because we try to do them without the aid of the Holy Spirit. We don't have to try to carry the burdens that life brings, for God has given us an invitation to cast all our cares upon Him, for He cares for us. We are told that if we are weary from the burdens that we are carrying to "Take His yoke upon us, learn of Him; for He is meek and lowly in heart: and we will find rest unto our souls. For His yoke is easy, and His burden is light." His Holy Spirit is waiting to lead you today; you do not have to try to figure it out today on your own. Trust Him now.

Daily Prayer

Father God, I place all of my cares upon you; please help me never to get ahead of you, in Jesus' Name, Amen.

FAITH TO BELIEVE AND TRUST

"Now faith is the substance of things hoped for, the evidence of things not seen."

Hebrews 11:1 (KJV)

Faith makes all things possible; it makes things that are not seen available; it makes the impossible possible. James makes it clear that faith without works is dead, being alone. The Hebrew writer declared: "Without faith it is impossible to Him: for he that cometh to God must believe that He is, and that He is a rewarder of them that diligently seek him." Faith is not wishing but evidence one has that what he/she is hoping for will come to pass. The Lord Jesus declared: "If ye have faith as a grain of mustard seed, ye shall say unto this mountain, Remove hence to yonder place; and it shall remove." Walk today by your faith and not by sight to the best of your abilities; it will produce great benefits.

Daily Prayer

Father God, help me today to grow my faith so that I may walk by my faith and not by sight, in Jesus, Amen.

BEYOND NATURAL SIGHT

"And Elisha prayed, and said, Lord, I pray thee, open his eyes, that he may see..."

2 Kings 6:17 (KJV)

Apostle Paul declared: "But as it is written, Eye hath not seen, nor ear heard, neither have entered into the heart of man, the things which God hath prepared for them that love Him. But God hath revealed them unto us by His Spirit: for the Spirit searcheth all things, yea, the deep things of God." In other words, what God has for us cannot be seen with the natural eye and can only be revealed through the Holy Spirit. There are always more for you than are against you; for "greater is He that is in you, than he that is in the world." This is what Elisha prayed for God to do for the young man, that God would open his eyes to see just how many were on their side. God did this, and he saw that the mountains were full of horses and chariots of fire round about them. God has your victory already assured.

Daily Prayer

Father God, thank you for revealing to me what you have planned for me and not allowing me to walk by what I see, in the Name of Jesus, Amen.

HE KEEPS US

"Set a watch, O Lord, before my mouth; keep the door of my lips."
Psalms 141:3 (KJV)

To be best of your abilities, be diligent to watch the words that you speak on today, remembering that "death and life are in the power of the tongue." Yes, out of your mouth can proceed blessings or curses, all according to the words that you speak. The Psalmist declared: "I will meditate also of all thy work, and talk of thy doings." This is a great place for you to start each day, meditating on what God has done and then speaking what you need Him to do for you each day. Your words can literally cause things to live or not materialize. That's the power of your words, your speech, or your talk. Speak life, speak positive, speak what you need today.

Daily Prayer

Father God, help me to guard my tongue and only speak what will cause blessings and increase in all that concerns me.

HIS WORD/PROMISES NEVER FAIL

"Blessed be the Lord, that hath given rest unto His people Israel, according to all that He promised: there hath not failed one word of all His good promise, which He promised by the hand of Moses His servant."

1 Kings 8:56 (KJV)

Y ou can rest assured that everything God has promised you will come to pass. Not one of His words has ever failed, and it never will. Samuel declared: "As for God, His way is perfect; the word of the Lord is tried: he is a buckler to them that trust in Him." The Hebrews writer declared: "Wherein God, willing more abundantly to shew unto the heirs of promise the immutability of His counsel, confirmed it by an oath: that by two immutable things, in which it was impossible of God to lie, we might have a strong consolation, who have fled for refuge to lay hold upon the hope set before us." You can stand on what God has said, He cannot lie.

Daily Prayer

Father God, thank you for leading me today according to your promises and will for my life, in the Name of Jesus, Amen.

OUR HELP IS IN HIM

"O our God, wilt thou not judge them? For we have no might against this great company that cometh against us; neither know we what to do: but our eyes are upon thee."

2 Chronicles 20:12 (KJV)

No matter who is against you, God is for you. Regardless of the battle, greater is He that is in you than he that is in the world. Look to the hills from whence cometh your help, all your help comes from the Lord. No matter what you are currently enduring, declare as the Psalmist did: "Mine eyes are ever toward the Lord; for He shall pluck my feet out of the net." Keep your spiritual eyes fixed upon the Lord, regardless of the surroundings or condition. Your help is available today; keep looking to the hills, God is always a present help for and to you. He will not delay or miss His appointment with you. Cast all your cares upon Him, for He cares for you.

Daily Prayer

Father God, I look to you for all my need and for all that I will attempt to do, in the Name of Jesus, Amen.

NOTHING IS TOO HARD FOR OUR GOD

"Is anything too hard for the Lord?..."

Genesis 18:14 (KJV)

The request cannot be too big; the need cannot be too great; the battle cannot be too difficult that God cannot handle. None is greater than our God, so today you can be assured that nothing will confront you that is too difficult for God to allow you to overcome. He is able to do exceeding abundantly above all that you can ask for on today. Don't be afraid or hesitant to go to Him in prayer for what you need. He will always be more than enough. All that you may face today pales in comparison to God's power and grace. Cast all your cares upon Him, for not only does He care for you, but His love for you is unconditional and His mercy endureth forever. Ask today for all that you need, for nothing that you can ask is too hard for Him to do.

Daily Prayer

Father God, thank you for always being more than enough and for always providing all my need in the Name of Jesus, Amen.

ALWAYS LEAVES US EXAMPLES

"For whatsoever things were written aforetime were written for our learning, that we through patience and comfort of the scriptures might have hope."
Romans 15:4 (KJV)

God allows us to learn from all that we go through. He causes things to work together for our good and also for His glory. Apostle Paul declared: "And not only so, but we glory in tribulations also: knowing that tribulation worketh patience; and patience, experience, and experience, hope." Patience is a learning tool. Used correctly, it will benefit us every time. Try, as hard as it may be, never to be impatient because of a perceived delay; patience will cause increase if we do not lose faith. Yesterday is over; however, we should learn from the battles we engaged in, the attacks that we overcame, and the struggles that we conquered. All of our experiences will help us to develop hope, knowing that hope is essential to our faith. Trust Him today.

Daily Prayer

Father God, help me to learn from my experiences of yesterday and never to repeat the errors or mistakes, in the Name of Jesus, Amen.

HE HAS GIVEN HIS ANGELS

"And God sent me before you to preserve you a posterity in the earth, and to save your lives by a great deliverance."

Genesis 45:7 (KJV)

We are never at the mercy of the enemy or facing anything alone. The Psalmist declared: "Because thou hast made the Lord, which is my refuge even the most High, thy habitation; There shall no evil befall thee, neither shall any plague come nigh thy dwelling. For He shall give His angels charge over thee, to keep thee in all thy ways. They shall bear thee up in their hands, lest thou dash thy foot against a stone." The Prophet Joel declared: "And it shall come to pass, that whosoever shall call on the Name of the Lord shall be delivered: for in Mount Zion and in Jerusalem shall be deliverance, as the Lord hath said, and in the remnant whom the Lord shall call." Yes, He has sent His angels alone to oversee your walk today. Trust them for guidance.

Daily Prayer

Father God, thank you for giving your angels orders to help and assist me on today, in the Name of Jesus, Amen.

IT'S HIS TIME

"My times are in thy hand: deliver me from the hand of mine enemies, and from them that persecute me."

Psalms 31:15 (KJV)

Time belongs unto the Lord. It is in His hand; therefore, don't allow the time to cause you to move before the appointed time of the Father. God has an appointed time for all that concerns you. He is never late, never too early, but always on time. "To everything there is a season, and a time to every purpose under the heaven." Time is not an enemy; it is God's plan to His children, and He will use it to fulfill His promise to them. Nothing is done by God that is not according to His time, purpose, and plan. Your time is not in question, never was, and never will be. Rejoice today: God has you on schedule for an appointment with what He has prepared for you. Wait for Him.

Daily Prayer

Father God, help me to be mindful of your time and never take it for granted, in the Name of Jesus, Amen.

NOT AS THE WORLD DOES IT

"And be not conformed to this world: but be ye transformed by the renewing of your mind, that ye may prove what is that good, and acceptable, and perfect, will of God."

Romans 12:2 (KJV)

We are to focus on the Will of the Father, not our own. Jesus Himself declared: "I can of mine own self do nothing: as I hear, I judge: and my judgment is just; because I seek not mine own will, but he will of the Father which hath sent me." It's not what we want on today but what the Father has planned for us; therefore, our prayer should be according to His will in heaven for us on today. Paul taught that we cannot conform to the dictates of the world but renew our thinking and mindset so that we can be transformed to know what is the perfect will of God. Whatever you do according to His will, you can expect it to be successful. Trust Him.

Daily Prayer

Father God, please help me to do everything according to your will on today so that I can be pleasing unto you, in the Name of Jesus, Amen.

ALWAYS A FORGIVING GOD

"For thou, Lord, art good, and ready to forgive; and plenteous in mercy unto all them that call upon Thee."

Psalms 86:5 (KJV)

The Word declares: "(For the Lord thy God is a merciful God;) He will not forsake thee, neither destroy thee, nor forget the covenant of thy fathers which He sware unto them." God's mercy is everlasting, cannot be exhausted, and is freely given by God. Through Christ, God has forgiven us forever. It is a gift that we could never pay, work for, or any such thing. Apostle John declared: "If we confess our sins, He is faithful and just to forgive us our sins, and to cleanse us from all unrighteousness." The Psalmist declared: "Thou has forgiven the iniquity of thy people, thou hast covered all their sins." Grace is waiting today, waiting to restore, revive, and redirect you on today. This is not a license to sin but a guarantee that God will forgive if you ask. Blessings.

Daily Prayer

Father God, thank you for always making forgiveness available to me. Please let me not abuse this privilege but walk in righteousness, in Jesus' Name, Amen.

NOT BY HUMAN EFFORTS

"Then He answered and spake unto me, saying, This is the Word of the Lord unto Zerubbabel, saying, Not by might, nor by power, but by my spirit, saith the Lord of hosts."

Zechariah 4:6 (KJV)

It is through Christ that we live, move, and have our very existence. It's not by our own power, our own abilities, or our own strength; but it is through the Holy Spirit that our victories will be won. It's never about what we can do, for without Christ, we can do nothing. It is all based upon what God has done, is doing, and will do. It is always God's power that gives us the victory. The Prophet Samuel declared: "The God of my rock; in Him will I trust: He is my shield, and the horn of my salvation, my high tower, and my refuge, my saviour; thou savest me from violence." It will never be because of our abilities but God's Spirit that will cause us to triumph.

Daily Prayer

Father God, help me to wait on you for all that I need to do so that I will never attempt anything based upon my own abilities, in Jesus' Name, Amen.

VICTORY THROUGH HIM

"O sing unto the Lord a new song; for He hath done marvellous things: His right hand, and His holy arm, hath gotten Him the victory."

Psalms 98:1 (KJV)

The Prophet Moses declared: "But thou shalt remember the Lord thy God for it is He that giveth thee power to get wealth, that He may establish His covenant which He sware unto thy fathers, as it is this day." It's the Lord who makes all things possible for us, regardless of what it is. Remember, "Every good and every perfect gift comes from above, and comes down from the Father of lights, with whom is no variableness, neither shadow of turning." All our provisions, all our blessings, and all that we will ever obtain or receive comes from the Lord God. If it is good, it comes from the Lord. Don't worry today; it's God's pleasure to take good care of you.

Daily Prayer

Father God, thank you for directing me into the things that you have planned for me on today, in Jesus' Name, Amen.

MY HELPER

"Behold, God is mine helper: the Lord is with them that uphold my soul."
Psalms 54:4 (KJV)

Isaiah declared: "Fear thou not; for I am with thee: be not dismayed; for I am thy God: I will strengthen thee; yea, I will help thee; yea, I will uphold thee with the right hand of my righteousness." He further stated: "For the Lord God will help me, therefore shall I not be confounded: therefore have I set my face like a flint, and I know that I shall not be ashamed… Behold, the Lord God will help me; who is he that shall condemn me? Lo, they shall wax old as a garment; the moth shall eat them up." Our Helper on the earth is the Holy Spirit, and The Father has sent Him to help, comfort, and lead us. Let Him lead and help you today.

Daily Prayer

Father God, thank you for sending the Helper, the Holy Spirit, to assist me in all I need in the Name of Jesus, Amen.

RESTORED BY HIM

"I have seen his ways, and will heal him: I will lead him also, and restore comforts unto him and to his mourners."

Isaiah 57:18 (KJV)

God can restore you, pick you up, and start you on a path of righteousness again. Solomon declared: "A just man falleth seven times, but he rises back up again." Restoration is your inheritance, regardless of your past or current condition. No matter what you have gone through or what you have done, God is a restorer. He will mend your broken heart, lift up your bowed down head, and re-start you again. Never be afraid to come back to the Lord, for the Hebrew writer declared: "We come boldly unto the Throne of Grace to obtain mercy, to find grace to help in the time of need." He is not just the God of a second chance but of multiple chances through Christ Jesus.

Daily Prayer

Father God, thank you for restoration, regardless of my failures or shortcomings, in the Name of Jesus, Amen.

NEW DAY, NEW THINGS

"Thou has heard, see all this; and will not ye declare it? I have shewed thee new things from this time, even hidden things, and thou didst not know them."

Isaiah 48:6 (KJV)

Regardless of what did or did not happen on yesterday or in the past, today is your new day, a day for new beginnings. Yesterday is gone. Its challenges may linger on, but this is a new day. Yesterday's issues should not be front and center of your day. If they are, you will miss all the new opportunities that God has prepared for you on today. This is the day that the Lord hath made; rejoice and be glad in it. The enemy has no clue what God is going to do for you on today and cannot stop, block, or hold it up because only God knows what's coming next. Rejoice for the new mercies; rejoice for the new opportunities; rejoice for new favor, all available because of new mercies from the Father.

Daily Prayer

Father God, thank you for new mercies and favor on today. Please help me to walk upright in them all day, in the Name of Jesus, Amen.

EVERY SPIRITUAL BLESSING IS OURS

"Blessed be the God and Father of our Lord Jesus Christ, who hath blessed us with all spiritual blessings in heavenly places in Christ."

Ephesians 1:3 (KJV)

God has made all that heaven has available to us through Christ Jesus – everything. Declare today that all heaven has is mine today, not going to be, but mine right now. These blessings include, but are not limited to, promotions, healings, favor, increase, deliverance, and victory. The Psalmist declared: "You welcomed him back with success and prosperity. You placed a crown of finest gold on his head." What a testimony to what God has already done for us. You are blessed and highly favored, and it is yours all day. Receive it as done; heaven has already made sure that its blessings are available to and for you today.

Daily Prayer

Father God, thank you for making all of heaven's spiritual blessings available to me. Please help me to walk in a manner befitting of them, in Jesus' Name, Amen.

THE UNCONDITONAL LOVE OF GOD

"But God commendeth His love toward us, in that, while we were yet sinners, Christ died for us."

Romans 5:8 (KJV)

One of the most quoted verses in the entire Bible is John 3:16: "For God so loved the world, that He gave His only begotten Son, that whosoever believeth in Him should not perish, but have everlasting life." That's nothing but unconditional love; we didn't deserve it and were not worthy of it, but it was just His unconditional love for His creation. This love is so strong and real that Apostle Paul declared: "For I am persuaded, that neither death nor life, nor angels, nor principalities, nor powers, nor things present, nor things to come, nor height, nor depth, nor any other creature, shall be able to separate us from the love of God, which is in Christ Jesus our Lord." This is unconditional love, and it does not need an invitation to operate for you.

Daily Prayer

Father God, thank you for loving me unconditionally and never forsaking or leaving me, in the Name of Jesus, Amen.

POWER FROM ON HIGH

"Then He called His twelve disciples together, and gave them power and authority over all devils, and to cure diseases."

Luke 9:1 (KJV)

Satan can suggest, tempt, and offer unreal things to you; however, be assured that he has no power over your life, not now, nor will he ever have any over you. Luke declared: "Behold, I give you power to tread on serpents and scorpions and over all the power of the enemy: and nothing shall by any means hurt you." David declared: "And now shall my head be lifted up above mine enemies round about me: therefore will I offer in His tabernacle sacrifices of Joy; I will sing, yea, I will sing praises unto the Lord." Because the Lord Jesus triumphed over the enemy at Calvary, we have the same victory. Apostle Paul declared: "And having spoiled principalities and powers, He made a show of them openly, triumphing over them in it." He has made this power available to you on today. Trust Him.

Daily Prayer

Father God, thank you for giving me the power and authority over all the works of the enemy. Please never allow me to misuse this authority, in the Name of Jesus, Amen.

HE IS JUST A CALL AWAY

"I will call upon the Lord, who is worthy to be praised: so shall I be saved from mine enemies."

Psalms 18:3 (KJV)

God is always just a prayer away. The Prophet Samuel declared: "… and that bringeth me forth from mine enemies: thou also hast lifted me up on high above them that rose up against me: thou hast delivered me from the violent man." You can be assured that God knows your enemies and what they are attempting to do to you; however, be encouraged, for "greater is He that is in you than he that is in the world." He is an on-time God, and He will never be too late to deliver you. Fear not; "God has not given you the spirit of fear, but of power, and of love, and of a sound mind." Be encouraged today; you will not have to fight alone.

Daily Prayer

Father God, thank you for hearing me when I call upon you. Please help me to keep looking to the hill from whence my help comes, in Jesus' Name, Amen.

WITHOUT QUESTION, GOD IS FOR US

"For I have heard the slander of many: fear was on every side: while they took counsel together against me, they devised to take away my life. But I trusted in thee, O Lord: I said, Thou art my God."

Psalms 31:13-14 (KJV)

The enemy will surely gather together against you; however, the Prophet Isaiah stated: "Behold, they shall surely gather together, but not by me: whosoever shall gather together against thee shall fall for thy sake." This is a promise of deliverance from the Father, and nothing the enemy can do will change this promise. Decree today that no weapon that is formed against me will prosper, and every tongue that shall rise against me in judgement thou shalt condemn. The Prophet Samuel reminded us of God's sovereign deliverance when He declared: "And all this assembly shall know the Lord saveth not with sword and spear: for the battle is the Lord's, and He will give you into our hand." Rest in Him today.

Daily Prayer

Father God, I thank you for being my covering, my protection, and my guide today from all that would harm me, in the Name of Jesus, Amen.

WATCHING WHAT WE THINK

"For as he thinketh in his heart, so is he: Eat and drink, saith he to thee; but his heart is not with thee."

Proverbs 23:7 (KJV)

Our thinking drives our conversation, our actions, and even our relationships. We are and will be what we consistently think about. Thoughts become words, words become acts, and acts represent lifestyles. Yes, we will do what we consistently think about. Think positive, and positive will most likely come unto you. God will keep you in complete peace if you keep your mind on the things of God. Everything begins with and in the mind; therefore, guard your heart and mind that you will not allow any unprofitable words to be uttered out of your mouth. Think you can, believe you can, and declare and decree that you will in the Name of Jesus.

Daily Prayer

Father God, please help me to keep my mind on the things that are positive, effective, and godly as I go throughout the day, in the Name of Jesus, Amen.

WATCH AND PRAY

"Watch and pray, that ye enter not into temptation: the spirit is indeed is willing, but the flesh is weak."

Matthew 26:41 (KJV)

Jesus encouraged the disciples to pray because their spirits were willing to hear, obey, and follow the things of the Kingdom; however, the flesh is weak and never wants to do what is required of the Father. In the Book of Luke, the Lord declared: "And He spake a parable unto them to this end, that men ought always to pray, and not faint." Prayer is effective in strengthening our spiritual walk, our discernment, and our hearing what the Spirit is saying to us. James declared: "The effectual fervent prayer of a righteous man availeth much." Our testimony, our witness, and our faithfulness are all affected by our prayer life. Pray that we enter not into temptation today. God is waiting to answer your request.

Daily Prayer

Father God, help me to remember the importance and value of a consistent prayer life so that I can be able to resist the temptations of the enemy, in Jesus' Name, Amen.

GOD HAS MADE ROOM FOR US

"...and He called the name of it Rehoboth; and he said, For now the Lord hath made room for us, and we shall be fruitful in the land."

Genesis 26:22b (KJV)

The enemy cannot dictate what God does for you, where He does it, or how He does it. He is always the God who is more than enough. He does not need to fight for space for you. He can move when, where, and how He wants in order to bless you. God will make room for you, regardless of what he enemy tries or plans to do. You do not have to fight for space, so to speak, for God will make room for you, not because you deserve it but because of His unconditional love for you. He is El Shaddai, God Almighty, and nothing is too difficult for Him. Don't be discouraged if God allows the enemy to think he has won against you; it just may be that He is using the fight to make room for you where He wanted you all the time. Trust Him.

Daily Prayer

Father God, thank you for always making room for me, even when I don't understand at the time, in the Name of Jesus, Amen.

THE GREAT TEACHER

"I will instruct thee and teach thee in the way which thou shalt go: I will guide thee with mine eye."

Psalms 32:8 (KJV)

The Lord will never leave you comfortless, but He has sent the Holy Spirit along with the Word to comfort and teach you. The Bible states: "The steps of a good man are ordered by the Lord, and He delights in His way." You can rest assured that God will lead, guide, and direct you in the way that He would have you to go. All you have to do is to be sensitive to the leading of the Holy Spirit, and you will arrive at your God-ordained destination. Today, trust Him for all directions, decisions, and paths that you should take. Declare and decree today as the Psalmist did: "Cause me to hear thy lovingkindness in the morning; for in thee do I trust: cause me to know the way wherein I should walk; for I lift up my soul unto thee." Trust Him today for all you need.

Daily Prayer

Father God, thank you for teaching and leading me throughout the day, in the Name of Jesus, Amen.

GROWING OUR FAITH

"And straightway the father of the child cried out, and said with tears, Lord, I believe; help thou mine unbelief."

Mark 9:24 (KJV)

The enemy would love for you to walk in doubt and fear, thereby weakening your faith to believe God. As much as you can, feed your faith and starve your doubt; this is done through spending time in the Word. Remember, "Faith cometh by hearing, and hearing by the Word of God." You can't have faith without having the Word of God in your heart and mind. Doubt will sometimes try to get unto all of our minds; however, we need to declare as this father who said: "Lord, I believe, help thou mine unbelief." Strong faith can only happen with a strong desire to learn from the Word. If there is a lack of word, there will be always be a lack of faith. Again, feed your faith today, and stave any doubt that may try to attach itself to you.

Daily Prayer

Father God, help me to strengthen my faith so that I will not walk in unbelief, in the Name of Jesus, Amen.

FOR HIS GLORY

"Jesus answered, Neither hath this man sinned, nor his parents: but that the works of God should be made manifest in him."

John 9:3 (KJV)

Some of the things that we experience cannot be explained or understood by us. However, God works all things after the counsel of His own will. Regardless of the severity or length of the trial, tribulation, or situation, God will work all things – all things – after what He desires, not ours. We must always trust God and believe that every outcome will work out in our favor. Some things are only for God's glory; nothing you could have done could have caused it, but God decided to use you to manifest His glory in the situation. The Lord will get the glory out of your struggle, and you will have a testimony no matter what the situation may have been. Trust Him today for the outcome in every situation.

Daily Prayer

Father God, thank you for all that you do for me and for allowing your glory to be seen in all that I go through, in Jesus' Name, Amen.

ABIDING IN THE VINE

"If ye abide in Me, and my words abide in you, ye shall ask what ye will, and it shall be done unto you."

John 15:7 (KJV)

We are nothing without the Father. We can do nothing except we abide in Him. Our lives are totally dependent upon Him for everything that we do. With Christ, all things are possible; however, without Him, we can do nothing. Try to begin each day with "I can do all things through Christ who strengthens me." No matter the situation, no matter the problem, seek God's way and provisions first; "In all thy ways acknowledge God, and He will direct your paths." The Lord is asking that you remain attached to Him, and you will produce much fruit. Stay with, trust, and depend upon the Lord; and He will give you the desires of your heart. He will never cast you away; all you need to do is remain attached to Him.

Daily Prayer

Father God, please help me to remain attached to you so that I do not go astray in Jesus' Name, Amen.

WORSHIP THE LORD IN THE SPIRIT

"God is a Spirit: and they that worship Him must worship Him in spirit and in truth."

John 4:24 (KJV)

God is a Spirit and cannot be worshipped in the flesh. Your body is involved in the worship experience; however, you spirit is totally engaged and in charge of the moment. This is not a one-time moment or event, but a lifestyle. Your flesh will never want to cooperate; however, you must learn to overpower the emotions or feelings that will try to keep you from worshipping God in the spirit and in truth. You are a spirit being, living life in a physical body, trying to worship the Father in the spirit realm. This will take all of your mind and spirt to become a true worshipper. However, you just need to simply surrender your emotions and will to Him; He will lead you into worshipping Him.

Daily Prayer

Father God, please help me to have the heart of a true worshipper every day, in the Name of Jesus, Amen.

THE POWER OF HIS WORD

"By the Word of the Lord were the heavens made; and all the host of them by the breath of His mouth."

Psalms 33:6 (KJV)

Everything that was made in the earth was made by the Word of God. The Gospel of John declared: "In the beginning was the Word, and the Word was with God, and the Word was God. The same was in the beginning with God. All things were made by Him; and without Him was not anything made that was made." If we want the same results, we must speak the Word of God over our situations and circumstances. The Hebrews writer declared that He "upholds all things by the word of His power," meaning everything that is standing is standing on the power of the Word of God. Speak the Word today over all that concerns you, knowing that God is "watching over His Word to perform it." Trust Him.

Daily Prayer

Father God, help me to speak your Word over all that I face, knowing that you are watching over Your Word to perform it, in Jesus' Name, Amen.

NOTHING TOO BIG FOR THE LORD

"Ah Lord God! Behold, thou hast made the heaven and the earth by thy great power and stretched out arm, and there is nothing too hard for Thee."
Jeremiah 32:17 (KJV)

Trust and know that nothing is too difficult for the Lord to do on your behalf. No request is too big; no need is too great; nothing is too hard for God. Whatever you face today, God is able to help you. Cast all your cares upon Him, for He cares for you deeply. The moment is not too big, the situation is not too grave, and the request is not too much that God cannot see you through. "Ask, and it will be given unto you; see, and you will find it; knock, and it will be opened unto you." There is nothing too difficult for God to do for you; take Him at His Word and make your request known unto Him. He is always more than enough.

Daily Prayer

Father God, thank you for always being more than enough, regardless of what I face or encounter on today, in the Name of Jesus, Amen.

FOLLOWING HIS LEAD

"I have set the Lord always before me: because He is at my right hand, I shall not be moved."

Psalms 16:8 (KJV)

The Lord will guide us into all truths and make straight the path that we should travel. The Psalmist declared: "I will bless the Lord who guides me; even at night my heart instructs me. I know the Lord is always with me. I will not be shaken, for He is right beside me. No wonder my heart is glad, and I rejoice. My body rests in safety." What an awesome assurance and peace of trusting in the provisions and protection of the Lord. Decree today that "You will show me the way of life, granting me the joy of your presence and the pleasures of living with you forever." Let the Holy Spirit lead you throughout the day; He is waiting to do just that.

Daily Prayer

Father God, I thank you for leading and guiding me into the directions that you have purposed for me, in the Name of Jesus, Amen.

HE WILL REVIVE YOU

"The instructions of the Lord are perfect, reviving the soul. The decrees of the Lord are trustworthy, making wise the simple."

Psalms 19:7 (NLT)

You can revive yourself today by finding yourself a "now word" from God's Word. The Psalmist declared: "The instructions of the Lord are perfect, reviving the soul." The Word will give you new life, a new hope, a new outlook, a new understanding. Take God at His Word. It is "sweet to the taste, yea sweeter than honey to the mouth." It is a "lamp unto thy feet, and a light unto thy path." The soul is revived each time the Word of God is entered into the heart. King David declared: "The entrance of thy words giveth light; it giveth understanding unto the simple." Be sure to spend time in the Word today, meditate on it; and it will revive, restart, and energize your soul.

Daily Prayer

Father God, thank you for reviving me today through Thy Word. Help me to keep my focus on the instructions found in it, in the Name of Jesus, Amen.

KEPT BY THE LORD GOD

"The Lord will preserve him, and keep him alive; and he shall be blessed upon the earth: and thou wilt not deliver him unto the will of his enemies."
Psalms 41:2 (KJV)

The Lord will preserve your going out and your coming in. He is a keeper, a preserver, and a strong tower. No matter the enemy, no matter the attack, the Lord will keep you in times of trouble. When the enemy attacks you, the Lord has already assured us that "no weapon that is formed against you shall prosper." Yes, the Lord will preserve you; He will keep you alive; He will bless you and will not deliver you over to the will of your enemies. Decree today that "The Lord is my light, and my salvation; whom shall I fear? The Lord is the strength of my life; of whom shall I be afraid?" He will deliver you, keep you, and preserve you. Take Him at His word.

Daily Prayer

Father God, thank you for keeping me, preserving me, and keeping me from the attacks of the enemy, in the Name of Jesus, Amen.

ABUNDANTLY BLESSED BY THE LORD

"I will abundantly bless her provision: I will satisfy her poor with bread."
Psalms 132:15 (KJV)

It is the Lord's pleasure to bless and prosper you. In fact, the Lord spoke in Deuteronomy that "...the Lord shall make thee plenteous in goods, in the fruit of thy body, and in the fruit of thy cattle, and in the fruit of thy ground in the land which the Lord sware unto thy fathers to give them. The Lord shall open unto thee His good treasure, the heaven to give the rain unto thy land in his season, and to bless all the work of thine hand: and thou shalt lend unto many nations, and thou shalt not borrow." We can see from the aforementioned scriptures that God has promised to bless our provisions and make us prosperous. You can rest assured today that God is not asleep at the wheel but will be watching over you to protect, lead, and bless you

Daily Prayer

Father God, thank you for blessing the works of my hands and for blessing all that I have, in the Name of Jesus, Amen.

IT WILL HAPPEN WHEN HE WILLS IT

"For the vision is yet for an appointed time, but at the end it shall speak, and not lie: though it tarry, wait for it; because it will surely come, it will not tarry."

Habakkuk 2:3 (KJV)

Remember today that God has a time for all that concerns you. It will not be late nor early, but right on time. Don't allow delay to cause you to lose faith in what has been promised to you. He is always on time with His promises and will not delay. The Lord has a set time to deliver, bless, and increase your blessings. He has a planned time for you to be rewarded for your faithfulness. No matter what the enemy tries, wait for the Lord. Habakkuk declared: "And the Lord answered me, and said, write the vision, and make it plain upon tables, that he may run that readeth it. For the vision is yet for an appointed time, but at the end it shall speak and not lie: though it tarry, wait for it; because it will surely come, it will not tarry." Trust Him.

Daily Prayer

Father God, help me to wait patiently upon you for all my needs to be met, in the Name of Jesus, Amen.

ASSURED VICTORY

"But thanks be to God, which giveth us the victory through our Lord Jesus Christ."

1 Corinthians 15:57 (KJV)

Our victory, our deliverance, and our overcoming are not in question. God is not making things up as we go along. He declared in Jeremiah: "For I know the thoughts that I think toward you, saith the Lord, thoughts of peace, and not of evil, to give you an expected end." No, God is not moved or worried about your current condition or position. His plans are to prosper you and get you to your expected end. He further expressed this in Isaiah when He declared: "Declaring he end from the beginning, and from ancient times the things that are not yet done, saying, My counsel shall stand, and I will do all my pleasure." You will not be left to the will of man today. Praise God for your victory.

Daily Prayer

Father God, thank you for planning my victory even before the battle, declaring me a winner before the attack, in Jesus' Name, Amen.

MAKING OUR PATH PLAIN

"And I will make all my mountains a way, and my highways shall be exalted."

Isaiah 49:11 (KJV)

No matter the situation, God will make a way for you to complete the task that He has assigned for you today. He is able to even make a way in the wilderness; trust Him for clearing a path for you to complete the day successfully. The Lord will provide all that is necessary for you to overcome, conquer, and survive all that you need on today. King David declared: "For the Lord God is a sun and shield: the Lord will give grace and glory: no good thing will He withhold from them that walk uprightly." Throughout the day, you can be assured that "you shall not go out with haste, nor go by flight: for the Lord will go before you; and the God of Israel will be your rereward." He is making a path for you to travel safely today! Rejoice.

Daily Prayer

Father God, thank you for making my path clear and for making a way for me in all that I face, in the Name of Jesus, Amen.

SAVED BY THE HAND OF GOD

"Though I walk in the midst of trouble, thou wilt revive me: thou shalt stretch forth thine hand against the wrath of mine enemies, and thy right hand shall save me."

Psalms 138:7 (KJV)

God is always a present help in times of trouble. He will not forsake you when the battle gets hard. He will not run away from you when things get difficult. He will never abandon you when everyone else does. No matter how difficult things may be, no matter how you have struggled, no matter how you have stumbled or have even fallen, don't ever stop trying. The enemy will never have the upper hand on you in anything that you have to encounter because of him. You shall be victorious on today, not by your own power or understanding, but by His outstretched hands. Enjoy this benefit all day.

Daily Prayer

Father God, thank you for being my strong tower and for leading me in a path that leads to my victory, in Jesus' Name, Amen.

EVERY PURPOSE HAS A SET TIME

"I said in mine heart, God shall judge the righteous and the wicked: for there is a time for every purpose and for every work."

Ecclesiastes 3:17 (KJV)

God has a set time to favor you, deliver you, bless you, and lift you out of all that would harm you. The Psalmist declared: "Thou shalt arise, and have mercy upon Zion: for the time to favor her, yea the set time is come." He may not come when you want Him, but He is always on time. God can even change the time and season if He chooses to on your behalf. Nothing the enemy does can stop God from getting to you when it is your set time. Be assured that God knows what, when, where, and how to cause all things to work together for your good. It's not your decision nor anyone else's.

Daily Prayer

Father God, teach me to be sensitive the leading of the Holy Spirit on today, knowing that you have a set time for all that concerns me, in Jesus' Name.

LIVING ACCORDING TO FAITH

"For therein is the righteousness of God revealed from faith to faith: as it is written, The just shall live by faith."

Romans 1:17 (KJV)

We are told to walk by faith and not by sight, meaning we are to walk not according to what we see in the natural, but according to what we know is possible through the Word and believing that God is going to do what He has promised. Remember, "Faith is the substance of things hoped for, the evidence of things not seen." Attack everything today with faith, in faith, and by faith. To the natural man, the flesh, it will not make sense; however, we walk by faith and not by what we see with our natural eyes. Faith does not need all the facts but operates on the knowledge that God can do all that we can ask or think. You can trust God's faithfulness; He will not fail you.

Daily Prayer

Father God, help me to walk by my faith and not by what I see every day with my natural eyes, in the Name of Jesus, Amen.

A GIFT CALLED TODAY

"This is the day that the Lord hath made; we will rejoice and be glad in it."
Psalms 118:24 (KJV)

God did not give you today with yesterday in mind. Today was given to you for the now moments, now blessings, the now opportunities that He will make available to you. Today is not an enemy but a gift from the Father. His plans for you today are not based upon what you did or did not do on yesterday. Trust Him to provide your every need and to direct your steps throughout the day. His mercies are new every morning; therefore, each new day brings you a new dose of God's unfailing and everlasting mercy. Today is a gift. Be sure to unwrap it, embrace it, and use it to the glory of the Lord. Receive this gift today as one filled with blessings, favor, opportunities, grace, mercy, and God's continued unconditional love.

Daily Prayer

Father God, thank you for this gift called today. Please help me to take full advantage of its many opportunities to the fullest, in the Name of Jesus, Amen.

SPEAKING ONLY WHAT WE WANT AND NEED

"Thy Words have upholden him that was falling, and thou hast strengthened the feeble knees."

Job 4:4 (KJV)

Make a decree today that nothing negative or harmful will come out of my mouth on today, knowing that death and life are in the power of your tongue. Apostle Paul let us know that we shall reap what we sow, whether it is good or bad. If we speak negative, we will receive negative; if we speak positive, we will receive positive. Every Word is a seed, seeds that will come up and produce a harvest. Job declared: "Thou shalt decree a thing, and it shall be established unto thee." Today, speak what you need; speak what you want; speak what you believe can come to pass. Speak His Word today, for He is watching over His Word to perform it.

Daily Prayer

Father God, help me to put a guard on my mouth that I do not speak anything that is not according to your will for me on today, in the Name of Jesus, Amen.

HIS PURPOSE WILL FOREVER STAND

"Calling a ravenous bird from the east, the man that executeth my counsel from a far country: yea, I have spoken it, I will also bring it to pass; I have purposed it, I will also do it."

Isaiah 46:11 (KJV)

Whatever God has purposed for you on today will come to pass just as He purposed it, when He purposed it, and how He purposed it. No worries, no one is able to undo what He has promised you. No enemy is big enough, no force is strong enough, and no situation is able to make Him withdraw His purpose from you. The day may present various opportunities and challenges. However, God has a plan and purpose for both. Nothing will surprise Him or be too difficult for Him to solve. Rest assured that you will be provided all that you will need to handle, both the opportunities and the challenges that you will face today so that God's purpose can be fulfilled in you. Nothing can undo what He has purposed and promised you.

Daily Prayer

Father God, thank you for always fulfilling your plan and purpose in my life. Help me never to walk contrary to either one, in the Name of Jesus, Amen.

www.ingramcontent.com/pod-product-compliance
Lightning Source LLC
Chambersburg PA
CBHW030910090426
42737CB00007B/147